PEACE FOR A PALESTINIAN

*One Woman's Story
of Faith amidst War in the Holy Land*

SAHAR QUMSIYEH

DESERET
BOOK

SALT LAKE CITY, UTAH

*To all the amazing people along my path who
have helped me become the person I am.*

Library of Congress Cataloging-in-Publication Data

Names: Qumsiyeh, Sahar B., author.
Title: Peace for a Palestinian : one woman's story of faith amidst war in the holy land / Sahar B. Qumsiyeh.
Description: Salt Lake City, Utah : Deseret Book, 2017. | Includes bibliographical references and index.
Identifiers: LCCN 2017040436 | ISBN 9781629723952 (paperbound : alk. paper)
Subjects: LCSH: Qumsiyeh, Sahar B. | Mormon converts—Personal narratives. | Palestinian Arabs—Biography.
Classification: LCC BX8695.Q86 A3 2017 | DDC 289.3092 [B] —dc23
LC record available at https://lccn.loc.gov/2017040436

Printed in the United States of America
Lake Book Manufacturing, Inc., Melrose Park, IL

10 9 8 7 6 5 4 3 2 1

CONTENTS

FOREWORD

Every day we can find evidence that hatred, violence, and vengeance abound in a world that appears to be forgetting God. In particular, the Middle East has become almost synonymous with retaliation, bloodshed, and distrust. In our prayers for peace in the ugly, complicated, and decades-old conflict between the Israelis and the Palestinians, we may naively conclude that God is on one side of the conflict and therefore the other side is an enemy of God. Such simplistic observations cease once we become acquainted with individuals who self-identify as Palestinian.

Those of us who know and love the Bible may develop a natural bias against Palestinians by equating the "Israel" of the Bible with the modern State of Israel. Knowing about the covenant that the Lord made with the twelve tribes of Israel in antiquity, including a land inheritance, we may unwittingly assume that this modern nation-state retains the same God-given right to control that land, no matter the cost. The scriptures teach us otherwise. The people of God are those whom He justifies. They live and embrace the gospel of Abraham. They love God with all their heart and might and their neighbors as themselves. As the Apostle Paul astutely observed, "They are not all Israel, which are of Israel" (Rom. 9:6), and as Nephi taught, "The Lord esteemeth all flesh in one; he that is righteous is favored of God" (1 Ne. 17:35).

In a landmark discourse to BYU students back in 1979, President Howard W. Hunter, then a member of the Quorum of Twelve Apostles, applied the Book of Mormon prophet Nephi's teachings to warn us against categorically discounting an entire nation, people, or race. He taught, "All men are invited to come unto [Christ] and all are alike unto him. Race makes no difference; color makes no difference; nationality makes no difference. . . . No nation or people or individual could expect to be favored above another. . . . We need to discover the supreme truth that indeed our Father is no respecter of persons. Sometimes we unduly offend brothers and sisters of other nations by assigning exclusiveness to one nationality of people over another. . . . [W]ords from the lips of the Master know no national boundaries; they are not limited to any race or culture." ("All Are Alike Unto God," *1979 BYU Speeches of the Year,* 32–35). President Hunter's direct and merciful message was a reminder that we mourn with those who mourn, feel sympathy with those who suffer, and avoid unconditionally taking sides in international conflicts. We may count Muslims, Jews, Christians, and those without affiliation with any religion among our friends.

The backdrop of this book is the Palestinian–Israeli conflict, but it is not a book about politics or government. It is a book about one Palestinian woman's remarkable experiences and choices to find hope and peace, kindled and fed by her faith in Jesus Christ, all while the political turmoil has continued to rage. Healing and peace are possible only through the perfect love of the Redeemer of the world.

Sahar Qumsiyeh is a Palestinian woman who was born in Jerusalem and grew up in Beit Sahour, close to Bethlehem. Brigham Young University offers a few scholarships each year to Palestinians. Without knowing anything about BYU, the state of Utah, or the LDS Church, Sahar accepted one of these scholarships to pursue a master's degree in statistics. While enrolled at BYU, Sahar joined the Church despite strong disapproval from her family and friends. Her story is, therefore, an invitation to better attune ourselves with a staggering percentage of people in the world who live in grave danger, deprivation, and hopelessness every day. By coming to know Sahar through her story, we may identify more readily and compassionately with those from any land whose lives are perpetually under siege.

I first met Sahar in the summer of 1999, when I became her visiting teacher in the Jerusalem Branch of the Church. I was in the Holy Land that year as a faculty member at BYU's Jerusalem Center for Near Eastern Studies. I had recently completed my doctoral dissertation that considered modern Palestinian families in the West Bank and Gaza Strip. My master's degree focused on the history, culture, and literature of the same land, albeit in antiquity. Together, these two degrees immersed me in a world of complex history and relationships in a land with a footprint about the size of the state of New Jersey.

As her visiting teachers, my companion and I typically visited with Sahar on the Sabbath at the BYU Jerusalem Center right after our worship services. I have not forgotten the day when Sahar invited us to come to her home in Beit Sahour for dinner. With our US passports, my companion and I easily passed through the checkpoint to drive to her home where she lived with her parents.

Her mother and older sisters joined Sahar to greet us. They prepared a banquet and were overwhelmingly hospitable to us as strangers in their home. I was curious to know what life was like for Sahar's mother when she was growing up in Palestine and how life had changed for her since 1948, when the State of Israel was created on land that had for centuries been owned and farmed by Palestinians. I asked several questions and they all replied graciously. During that visit, I noted the respect that this matriarch received from her daughters. I also learned that each of them, mother included, was highly educated and each placed a high value on education for her children—sons and daughters. I began to receive a glimpse of Sahar's rich ancestry, a family who for generations had inhabited the land amid numerous invasions and rule under various foreign despots, all the while retaining their identity as Palestinian Christians.

When I asked how they felt about Sahar's conversion to the LDS Church, Sahar's mother told me it was hard to see her daughter affiliate with an organization that is anti-Palestinian and pro-Israeli. My heart broke. I told her about our doctrine that all are alike unto God and that I had a deep love and respect for many Palestinians and Israelis that I knew personally through my research and teaching there. I told her that the God I worship would not condone the atrocities that her people had suffered. My visiting teaching companion verbalized something similar about her beliefs and perceptions, but I could tell that this strong and articulate matriarch, who had seen so much tragedy over the years, did not believe us. We belonged to an American church in her mind, and America was pro-Israel, so we must be, too.

Soon after I returned home from my BYU assignment in Jerusalem, Sahar began sending emails about her week, including the hardships she faced every week to travel to church at the Jerusalem Center. That was the first time I knew what a sacrifice in time and physical safety she made just to travel less than ten miles to participate with fellow members in a church service. Her messages of faith and hope every Christmas and Easter were especially poignant because of her expressions of joy and peace borne out of an unwavering covenant to follow Jesus Christ. I began saving and collecting those emails, not knowing what I wanted to do with them. I only knew that they were making a difference to my own sense of commitment to my faith. About five years later, Sahar sent me a working copy of her life story she had been writing. I was spellbound when I learned more about her, her siblings and parents, and her grandparents. That is when I knew she needed to write her story for many, many more to read.

Numerous changes have occurred in Sahar's life since then. She is now a math professor at BYU–Idaho. Several setbacks and opportunities have precluded her from writing this book until recently. Two things, however, have not changed during this window of time. Threats against any possible peace settlement in the Holy Land are as intransigent as ever. At the same time, Sahar's commitment to and love for her Savior continue to be rock solid. She has found the path to peace and healing while storms of hatred and violence continue to rage around her. Her discovery is not exclusive to her. Each of us may find the solution for ourselves. Sahar's story tells us that peace through the Prince of Peace is possible for all of us.

CAMILLE FRONK OLSON
April 19, 2017

PROLOGUE

"Go home! You can't enter Jerusalem! Go back!" the soldier at the checkpoint screamed at me. This soldier who had invaded my country was now telling me that I was denied access to the city of my birth. I tried to form angry words to respond to his unjust act but was halted by the words of the Savior echoing in my ear: "Love your enemies."

Memories flashed through my mind of times when I had seen these soldiers demolish homes of my relatives, beat people until their bones were broken, arrest family members, and prevent me from going to church in Jerusalem and partaking of the sacrament. Images came to my mind of those soldiers invading my sister's home in the middle of the night, terrorizing her children, and arresting her husband and keeping him in jail with no charge for months.

Another distinct picture then formed in my mind. This picture was of Isaac, a fellow student at Bethlehem University. I saw him right after he was shot by an Israeli soldier. I saw the bullet hole in his head. All of a sudden, I was again able to smell the tear gas in the air and feel the sad atmosphere at the university that day in 1987. We all stood there and watched as Isaac fought for his life, because the soldiers wouldn't allow him to be taken to a hospital. After his death, I remembered Isaac's body getting thrown in a hole by the soldiers, preventing his family from giving him a proper burial.

Anger and hate filled my soul, and I thought, *How could the Lord expect me to love these soldiers? Is that even possible? After what I have seen some of the soldiers do, He could not possibly expect me to love them!* The words came again, now more real to my mind: "Love your enemies." The Lord's voice was clearly directed at me.

I am a Palestinian Arab. I was born and raised in Palestine, a place of constant conflict. Yet by following the Savior, the Prince of Peace, I have been able to find true peace, joy, and forgiveness. When I started to follow Him, my life changed—from despair to hope, from depression to joy, and from darkness to light. We all face challenges in our lives—some more extreme than others—but the source of peace and comfort is the same for all of us.

Through the Savior and His Atonement, I have learned that not only is it possible to love our enemies but also to live with peace in a country of turmoil. The Savior can heal all wounds, but most important, He can heal our hearts. When we follow Him, all things become possible.

I love the Holy Land. It has always been a land that attracts visitors from all over the world. Those who were born here, like me, are forever connected to this land. I love the people, the hills, and the beautiful wildflowers that cover the rocky landscape in springtime. I call the land Palestine, even though many refer to it as Israel. I hope that as you take this journey with me, you will understand why Palestine is a name that is dear to my heart. I was born Palestinian and will always be Palestinian, even if others do not recognize this as a valid nationality. Whatever the name, this part of the world is where Jesus was born, where He walked the streets and taught the people, where He lived, suffered, and died. It is also the place where He broke the bands of death and rose triumphant from the darkness of the tomb. It is the geographical location that is theologically central to three world religions: Judaism, Christianity, and Islam.

You may have been led to take sides regarding the current conflict between Palestinians and Israelis. You may have been led to believe that one side of the conflict is at fault. Some of you may even have been led to have some feelings of hatred toward people of certain ethnic origins or religion. I invite you to set those feelings aside and fill your heart with love.

In these few pages, as I share my experiences, I hope I can take your hand and help you live each experience with me. As we walk together across the pages of this book, I want you to see, through my eyes, how the Savior's light shines in the darkest and hardest of times. As you begin to see His light and His hand in my life, I hope you will recognize that same light in your life as well. Peace and joy come as we follow the Savior of the world, who offers us a special kind of peace: "Peace I leave with you, my peace I give unto you: not as the world giveth, give I unto you. Let not your heart be troubled, neither let it be afraid" (John 14:27).

After years of drowning in despair resulting from the political conflict and turmoil in my country, I found peace. To help you see how peace can triumph even while the battle still rages, I want to take you on a journey through the life of a Palestinian Mormon. I invite you to my home in the Holy Land to share my culture and my people's history. Through sharing some of the trials I've faced I can serve as a witness of the glorious miracles that have followed. Peace occurs one person at a time. My hope is that by sharing my story of finding peace, others will be inspired to discover that peace is possible for them as well.

Chapter 1

NURTURE

"Suffer little children to come unto me, and forbid them not: for of such is the kingdom of God" (Luke 18:16).

"دعوا الأطفال يأتون إليّ ولا تمنعوهم: لأن لمثل هؤلاء ملكوت السماوات." (لوقا ١٨: ١٦)

"Come in," said the boy. The young woman who would become my mother, Fawz, had just arrived at the house to pick up her friend on her way to church one Sunday. Fawz objected, "Please call your sister; we have to go. We are late for church."

"But I need help with my math," the boy protested.

It was her friend's brother, and because of her passion for teaching, Fawz was unable to resist this request for help, so she stepped inside. Fawz had started teaching at a school after graduating from the Teachers' Training College, and she loved teaching.

My mother was one of the few Palestinian women to even go to school. When she was a student, her class at the Teachers' Training College in Jerusalem had one student from each town. She was chosen to represent the Bethlehem area. Her desire for an education was so great that she often risked going to school despite dangers that arose during the Second World War. The bus that took her to school was often shot at, but she was still determined to get an education. One of her classmates, Hayah, was killed in the village of Deir Yassin in 1948, when the Israeli army massacred almost everyone in that village. Hayah was shot along with all the children she was teaching at the time.

Fawz persevered and excelled in her class despite the difficult times. After the shootings in Deir Yassin, the Israeli soldiers would drive around Palestinian villages in their army jeeps and announce on loud speakers, "If you don't leave, we will do to you what we did in Deir Yassin." Many Palestinians at the time chose to leave and lost their right to return to their villages and towns; they became homeless refugees. My mother and her family stayed, assured by the fact that living close to the holy city of Bethlehem would give them some protection. Fawz's family had just moved to Bethlehem. Her family at the time included her parents, Issa and Milia Atallah, and her seven siblings.

As my mother helped this demanding boy with his mathematics, she was eager to finish so she and her friend would not be late for church. Her rush in helping the boy distracted her from the real reason that he had asked her to step inside. The reason was not mathematics homework; it was to introduce her to a young man, Botros, who was waiting inside. Botros was interested in Fawz and wanted to see her before he asked for her hand in marriage. He sat anxiously awaiting her arrival and focused his eyes on the door as Fawz entered. When she finally entered the house, Botros jumped up and introduced himself. Fawz briefly shook hands with him and quickly turned to the mathematics book. Botros examined this woman he had just met. She seemed to radiate goodness and beauty. He admired her beautiful blue dress, her dark hair, and her soft, dark complexion. He felt he had just met the woman who was to be his wife.

Because his father had passed away, Botros resorted to taking his oldest brother, Jeries, with him to Fawz's parents' house to ask for her hand in marriage. Jeries was a good friend of Issa, Fawz's father. After Botros and Jeries left, Fawz's father informed her of the wedding proposal. She was startled—she was not expecting it and had not considered marriage yet. Her father told her what a wonderful man Jeries was and insisted that since Botros came from a good family, he would make a good husband.

My father, Botros, was born on March 14, 1929, to a poor family. They lived in a town called Beit Sahour, a Christian town right next to Bethlehem. Beit Sahour is one of the few Christian towns in Palestine. It is about a ten-minute walk from the Church of the Nativity, the location traditionally considered to be where Christ was born. On the hills of Beit Sahour, over two thousand years ago, a few shepherds sat watching over their flocks at night. An angel appeared to them, informing them of the birth of the Savior of the world in Bethlehem, a nearby town. Those shepherds went with haste from Beit Sahour to Bethlehem to worship the Messiah, and they testified to others of Him.

Botros worked as a teacher in the boys' school in Bethlehem. His father, Hanna, died at a young age and left Botros's mother, Aziza, to raise seven children alone. Despite that, all of the children were well educated and had a good reputation in the community. Fawz accepted this sudden marriage proposal. Botros and Fawz were married on August 30, 1953.

Sadly, their first son, born a year later, died at birth due to a mistake committed by the midwife. Fawz was devastated. She held the lifeless, beautiful baby boy in her arms and cried. "Heavenly Father," she said, "please let me have another son soon. I don't care if he is ugly. I just want him to be a boy." Fawz had amazing faith. She often went to the Lutheran church, because her mother, Milia, was Lutheran. Even though her church attendance declined due to the demands of married life, she still had a strong faith in God.

Fawz found herself pregnant again shortly after her first baby was born. On December 19, 1955, she gave birth to another son, Maher. He was dark when he was born and not as good-looking as the first baby, but Fawz did not care. He was alive and a boy! She loved him instantly. Maher, my eldest brother, turned out to be very smart, with a passion for mathematics. It was his influence that later motivated me to pursue a degree in mathematics and eventually statistics. He is also great at fixing

Shepherds' Field in Beit Sahour.

things, especially computers. Sometimes he could simply look at my computer and it would start working again.

A year after that, my mother had another son, Mazin, on May 12, 1957. Mazin always had a love for animals. I remember him bringing animals, especially bats (his favorites), home to study. He loves working and keeping busy, so he does not like to waste a single minute. Mazin also likes to help others and has gone to many demonstrations advocating for those whose homes were about to be demolished by the Israeli army. He has been arrested many times due to his efforts. He has also helped secure funding for some Palestinians who needed medical care after gunshot wounds. In one of his books, *Sharing the Land of Canaan,* he outlines the history of the Palestinian–Israeli conflict and shares facts that may have been neglected by others. He clarifies that peace can be possible only if it is based on maintaining human rights and equality. An interesting story about Mazin is that when he was almost two years old, he fell out of the window from the second floor. He walked away without a scratch.

Eleven months after Mazin was born, on April 30, 1958, Fawz had another son, Walid. Walid is a person with a very kind heart. He thinks of others before he thinks of himself. Being the youngest of three boys, he often found himself doing a lot of the chores. When the three brothers were in college, they shared a room. One day Walid went shopping and cooked a nice meal for his two brothers. After they finished eating, Walid thought it only fair that his brothers do the dishes since he had done the shopping and the cooking. Maher and Mazin refused to do the dishes. Walid proceeded to throw the dishes out of the window because he was so upset that they wouldn't help him. I still remember the cute cards Walid used to send me when he was away at college. He always told me that he loved and missed me. Those cards made me feel very special.

Two years after Walid was born, my mother found herself pregnant again. She already had three sons under the age of four, and she was also working. She really did not want any more children, but my sister, Suhair, came along on May 13, 1960. Suhair was meant to be born and stay healthy, because she would become the strength of our family. When she was one year old, she contracted a disease that the doctors said would leave her paralyzed. They said there was no cure to the disease and that there was nothing they could do. My mother prayed and promised Heavenly Father that if He cured her daughter, she would light a candle in St. George's church every year. Suhair was miraculously healed and showed no signs of paralysis after that. To my parents, she is a favorite child. She always serves them and worries about their needs. Suhair was like a second mother to me, and I cried when she left home to marry. She now works as a schoolteacher and comes home after work to cook for her whole family (including her married son and his family), and she babysits her granddaughters every day. As soon as her daughter-in-law comes home from work and picks up her children, Suhair rushes to my mother's house to check on her. She plays games with my mother to keep her from getting bored.

Two years after Suhair was born, my mother became pregnant once more. Samar came along on October 12, 1962. She is the most beautiful of all my siblings. She had blond hair and green eyes when she was a baby. Her hair is darker now, but she remains as beautiful as ever.

Growing up, I always looked forward to holidays and weekends because I knew Samar would have time to play with me. Samar is now a nurse and a certified midwife. She has helped bring countless babies into this world. She always wanted to become a math teacher instead of a nurse, but I feel that she was meant to be a nurse. I have seen her take care of her patients and show them a kind of love that they didn't normally experience. She cares about others and is really good at what she does.

Nine years after Samar was born, my mother noticed that her children were slowly leaving the house. They were growing up too fast. So she wanted another child to keep her company in her old age. She was almost forty years old then, and she didn't know if she even could get pregnant, but she did. She hoped this sixth child would be a girl to even the score, since she had three boys and two girls. She awaited the birth of this child—me—with great anticipation.

Early in the morning on April 29, 1971, Fawz began bleeding severely. Seeking better medical care, my father rushed her to a doctor in Jerusalem. The twenty-minute drive seemed too long as both of my parents feared for the life of their baby. Fawz, getting weaker due to the loss of blood, managed to get out of the car as it stopped in front of the doctor's office. She gazed up the long staircase that led to the doctor's office on the second floor. Leaning and relying on her husband's strong arms, she made the slow ascent to the top of the stairs. The couple looked at each other in disappointment and fear when the doctor told them to leave. He would not accept Fawz as a patient because, he said, he had had another patient with the same condition recently, and that patient had died. It would be bad for his reputation to have another similar case. The reality and severity of her situation suddenly dawned on Fawz, and she nearly lost what little strength she had left.

Botros lifted Fawz up, giving her courage and strength, and took her to Al-Maqasid hospital on the Mount of Olives, where the doctors performed a C-section. My father was thrilled to hear me cry in the operation room, because he had been worried that I would not survive. However, after the operation, despite all their efforts, the doctors were unable to stop my mother's bleeding. The doctors prepared my parents for the worst. If the bleeding didn't stop soon, my mother would lose her life.

My mother lay on a hospital bed, fighting for her life, with her newborn baby nearby. My father was busy trying to find donors to give blood to save my mother's life. After exhausting all other sources, he paid some tourists to donate blood. Because the blood was not tested properly, some of it caused an allergic reaction and made my mother's condition worse. She was covered in a red rash and was weak and barely able to move. As my father approached her hospital bed later that day, she looked at him with her frail eyes and told him that she was going to die. "Botros, you have to marry Olgha. She would be a good mother to our children. Promise me you will marry her after I die," she said.

My father looked at my mother and said, "You are not going to die. You have to live."

With disbelief, my weak mother persisted, "Just promise me, please." My father nodded reluctantly, trying to stop tears from rolling down his face. He had to remain strong, for his wife and for his six children.

The nurse brought me close to my mother, who looked at my tiny, helpless body and wondered what would happen to me. A new determination appeared in her eyes as she pleaded with the Lord, "Please help me live so I can raise this baby. Help me not die before she grows up and gets married." It was that determination and faith that helped my mother survive. She is convinced that her recovery commenced after that prayer. Today she is eighty-five years old and still strong and alert (I have not yet married, you see, and that must be why she is still alive).

Even though I was born in Jerusalem, my parents chose to list Beit Sahour as my birthplace. The changes that were occurring in my country made my family fearful of listing Jerusalem as my birthplace. They thought it might cause problems for me living with them in Beit Sahour.

The situation in my country has not always been as bad as it is today. I actually grew up during a time when things were relatively calm in Palestine. There were very few checkpoints, and we were allowed to travel freely to any part of our country.

Courtesy Akram Hilal.

Beit Sahour, town center.

Every Christmas and Easter all the Qumsiyeh family (a few hundred people) gather together. We dress up and meet together to wish everyone a merry Christmas. My uncles used to give us Christmas gifts—money—and we would run to the store and buy toys or candy. It was a fun time to spend with relatives and enjoy each other's company.

My family belonged to the Greek Orthodox church. This was the largest Christian denomination in the Bethlehem area. My father purchased a piece of land in Beit Sahour and then divided it into three parts. My uncle Yacoub bought one piece, and my cousin Jalal bought another. The house that my family built on our piece of land became our new home. When I was born, my family had just moved into this new three-bedroom home. We had one room that we called the boys' room (where my three brothers slept) and one room that we called the girls' room (where my sisters and I slept). The house had a nice, big garden with many fruit and olive trees. My father built swings for us, and we loved to play there while eating fruits from the garden. I can still taste the fresh figs, tangerines, and lemons. My favorite was eating lemons with salt. My mouth still waters as I think about eating those juicy lemons.

I always enjoyed being outside under the warm sun surrounded by

Uncle Jeries's house, where our family gathered together every Christmas.

Our street, including our house and my uncle's house.

olive trees and grass. I loved climbing our large olive trees and looking around. I felt superior and strong as I looked down from the top of our mighty olive trees. My favorite time of year was in the fall during the olive-picking season. I did not do much to help my family pick the olives, but I would climb trees and act like I was helping. It took our family of eight a whole day to pick the olives from one tree and clean the olives by removing the stems and leaves.

My family's house.

One of our lemon trees.

My mother was one of the first women in the area to work after marriage. She was the school principal of the only girls' school in Beit Sahour at the time. The school had only grades 1 through 4. When I was two, my mother taught me to read a few words. She would brag and show those who visited our house how her two-year-old daughter could read

From left to right: my father holding me, my sister Samar, my mother standing behind my cousin Rana—in our backyard before the fruit trees were planted.

the words *mom, dad, Maher,* and *Mazin.* When I was four years old, my mother didn't have anyone that could babysit me while she worked, so she would take me with her to school. She had me sit in the first grade with the other kids. I would often slip out of the classroom and play on the playground. I got to do what I wanted because, after all, my mother was the principal, and no one could say no to me. At the end of the school year, I took the first-grade exams and received the highest grade in the class. I was barely five years old, and my mother wanted me to repeat the first grade instead of moving up to the second grade with my friends. I, however, was not about to let that happen. How could I repeat the class when I was the best student? I moved up to the second grade.

My cousin Rana lived next door, and we were almost the same age. We spent every minute together when we were kids. We rode our bikes down the streets of Beit Sahour, up and down those hilly roads. We climbed hills and went into caves, exploring our surroundings and

Me (on left) and Rana (on right), roasting pinecones.

finding new animals and bugs. The smooth, white rocks on those hills were our resting places as we sat to eat snacks or gather poppies and other flowers in the spring. We accompanied my brother Mazin as he explored caves and studied bats, mice, and other animals. On colder days we sat on those hills by a fire and roasted pinecones and ate fresh roasted pine nuts.

Despite these beautiful excursions in nature and the fun times we spent on those Beit Sahour hills, my favorite places were far from Beit Sahour. The sea fascinated and relaxed me. I could spend hours sitting on the beach, listening to the sound of the waves hitting the rocks or reaching out to grab a handful of sand to take back to the sea. As a child, swimming in the sea, feeling the waves move my body around, and walking with the sand under my feet were activities I felt I needed in order to survive. Luckily, in spite of the long drive, my uncle Yacoub took us to Askalan beach (on the Mediterranean) often. Sometimes, we took long trips to Eilat along the Red Sea and watched the amazing fish that filled those beautiful, clear waters.

The Dead Sea was another place we visited often during the summer. Our family, including my uncles and their families, went to a place called Al-Fashkha near the Dead Sea. It had natural springs, and swimming in the crisp, clean water of those streams and rivers was life changing. We loved going there, and the night before we would go, we were so excited that we couldn't sleep. I still have dreams about being in that place again, watching the fish and crabs and feeling the freshness of the cool spring water.

I often reflect on those happy moments in my childhood. They were all taken away from me so fast. The laughter and carefree days of my childhood were soon replaced with fear. The situation began to get worse, and checkpoints and roadblocks started to separate us from those beautiful places that we had once known and loved.

A Day in My Life 1

Background: A journal entry from a hot day in August. I was working at the Arab American University near Jenin. I taught summer classes and was home in Beit Sahour visiting my family over the break after the summer session was over.

I enjoyed having a break from the daily summer classes I had to teach. I have done nothing during this break except rest, watch TV, and play cards with my family, and it was wonderful. Maybe I was lazy at times, but I feel I deserve some rest after a busy summer session. It was so hot in the classrooms every day and hard to even think. My students often looked like they were melting in the heat.

My father took his chemo today and he is not doing well. He will probably feel better in a few days though.

I made it to church three times this month. I didn't think I would make it there today, but sometimes it is amazing how the Lord interferes. The first checkpoint at the edge of town had been removed, so I was able to pass easily. The other checkpoint was completely closed (meaning they were not letting anyone through). The Israeli soldier there said anyone with a Bethlehem Identity card (like me) couldn't get out. Everyone just stood there (about 500 people) and tried to argue with the soldier, who was starting to get a little angry. I thought about climbing the hill, but everyone said that those who did climb the hill found soldiers on the top of the hill and were forced to turn back.

I decided I could avoid the whole mess at that checkpoint by going to Wad-El-Hummus. It is a dirt road that has been blocked by a pile of rocks by the Israeli army. I turned around and took a taxi all the way back to Bethlehem, then took one from there to Wad-El-Hummus. The taxi drove 40 miles per hour on that rocky dirt road. I felt I was sitting in a blender! I got to the pile of rocks and climbed it on foot to the other side. From there I took another taxi to Silwan (inside Jerusalem now). From Silwan, I took a bus all the way to Damascas Gate. There were many soldiers and police on the way, but we were not stopped. At Damascas Gate I got in a taxi that took me to the BYU Jerusalem Center.

The first half of the day was great because despite all obstacles, I made it to church on time. I was so happy about that. Nedy, who is not a member of the Church, gave a really great talk in sacrament meeting. She is such a sweet girl. I am sure she will join the Church in the Philippines, which is where she was heading on Tuesday to be reunited with her kids—whom she had not seen since they were babies—and with her husband.

After church, I promised Paul (an American) and Majeda (from Poland) that I would give them a tour of Bethlehem. I often gave tours to visitors who were either afraid of going to Bethlehem or did not know quite how to go. I actually got in trouble with the Ministry of Tourism because they thought I was charging people for my tours. They could not believe that I am giving tours so often without charging people for them. However, I simply loved being with members of the Church and loved giving everyone a chance to visit Bethlehem. Many came to the Holy Land and left without even going to Bethlehem. I felt their trip would be incomplete without visiting the best place in Palestine, so I wanted to give everyone that opportunity.

Paul, Majeda, and I headed towards Bethlehem. We tried to take a taxi from Damascas Gate to Bethlehem, a distance of about five miles. However, the taxi driver said he couldn't take me because I have a Bethlehem Identity card and don't have a permit that allows me to be in Jerusalem. He said transporting someone like me in his taxi is illegal. He said if the police were to catch him, they would take his car for 30 days and make him pay a 5,000 Shekel ($1,200) fine. Paul and Majeda could have gotten in the taxi and made it to Bethlehem in about fifteen minutes. But they were willing to go with me the back long route.

We walked back to the bus stop and took a taxi that took us to Bethany and from there to "The Gate." The Palestinian city of Bethany has been split into two pieces by the Separation Wall, and there is only a small gate that is left as an opening in the Wall to go from one side of the town to the other.

City of Bethany, showing the separation wall.

Israeli soldiers monitor the gate and allow only specific people through. We got off the taxi and walked through the Gate with no problem. From there we took a taxi to the center of town and looked for a taxi to Bethlehem. People laughed at us and said, "There is no road to Bethlehem, you will need to take a taxi to the checkpoint and then hope the soldiers will let you walk through on foot." We were tired and sweaty by then, so we were relieved to find a taxi to take us to the checkpoint. This was all happening in August and the temperature was over 100 degrees Fahrenheit.

The soldier at the checkpoint agreed to let me in, since I had a Bethlehem identity card, but looked at Paul's American passport and said, "Where is your identity card?" Since the soldier could not speak English well, we could not explain that Paul was American and didn't have a Palestinian identity card, nor an Israeli one. The soldier got angry because he demanded an identity card and Paul did not know what to give him. Innocently, Paul handed the soldier his American driver's license, but that did not satisfy the soldier. In broken English, the soldier asked Paul where he lived. Paul told him that he was here for a short while and that he lived in Haifa. "Go back to Haifa," the soldier demanded.

I felt bad that after all I had put Paul and Majeda through, they would now have to turn around and go back to Jerusalem. They had never been to Bethlehem and were so excited to visit the place where the Savior was born. We tried to argue with the soldier and convince him to let them through, but he yelled, "The checkpoint is closed. Go back."

Sadly, I knew there was another checkpoint after this one and passing through this one did not mean we would be able to pass through the next one. I told Paul and Majeda that they had two options. First option, go down the hill in the heat, walk up to the other checkpoint, and try their luck there. If that checkpoint did not let them in, they would have to climb the hill and go back to Jerusalem the way they came. Second option, go back the exact same route and back to Damascas Gate in Jerusalem and take a taxi to the north Bethlehem checkpoint, which should let them through for sure. I said I would meet them on the other side of that checkpoint.

They chose option 1 and wanted to walk down the hill, so off we went. There were five Palestinian women with luggage and kids who were on their way back home after traveling abroad. They walked down the hill with us. There were babies and little children rolling on the rocks, falling and slipping. I felt bad for those poor women, but they had no choice except go down the hill to get home.

Luckily, when we got to the second checkpoint we were allowed through and we took a taxi from there to Bethlehem. The whole trip took over two hours. Knowing that the actual distance from Jerusalem to Bethlehem is about five miles, this was surely too difficult for my friends. Paul and Majeda actually had the adventure of their life, it seems. They told me that people discouraged them from coming to Bethlehem and told them it is not safe. But they were amazed when we finally got there. Paul kept commenting, "Wow, it is so peaceful here and so quiet."

LEBANON

SYRIA

Mediterranean Sea

West
Bank

Gaza
Strip

ISRAEL

JORDAN

EGYPT

Gulf of
Aqaba

Agricultural gates
Frequency of opening
⊗ Daily *
✸ Seasonal **
✖ Seasonal Weekly ***

West Bank Barrier
—— Constructed
········ Under Construction
········ Projected

▮ Israeli Settlements
  Behind the Barrier
▮ Area Behind the Barrier

* Generally open 15-60 minutes; 3 times/day.

** Open daily during olive harvest only

*** Open 3 times/day; 1-3 days/week; during
olive harvest

Mediterranean Sea

West Bank

Jenin

Tubas

Tulkarm   Jubara

Qedumim
Finger

Qalqilya   Nablus

Ari'el
Finger

Salfit

Bil'in

Ramallah

Jericho

No Man's
Land

1949 Armistice (Green Line)   Biddu Gates

Al Walaja   Jerusalem   Ma'ale
                          Adumim
                          Settlement
                          Bloc

ISRAEL   Bethlehem

Gush
Etzion
Settlement
Bloc

Hebron

JORDAN

Jordan River

International Boundary

Dead Sea

1949 Armistice (Green Line)

Kilometres
0   5   10

If I had not been with Paul and Majeda that day, they would have gotten on a taxi in Jerusalem and easily gotten to Bethlehem in about fifteen minutes. But they were traveling with a Palestinian, and that made things super complicated, it seemed. I know some Palestinian women that make this long trek to Jerusalem every day to sell their fruits and vegetables. They pay at least 30 Shekels ($7) each way. How many pounds of produce can they carry, how much can they sell? They make very little money, but they have no choice and no other source of income.

I am grateful that we don't have a curfew these days in Bethlehem. My friend Abeer, who lives in Nablus, told me they have been under curfew for many days. Today, the Israeli soldiers allowed them to leave their homes to buy supplies for a few hours, but then the curfew was back.

Chapter 2

IDENTITY

"I am a child of God, and he has sent me here, Has given me an earthly home With parents kind and dear." (Hymns, no. 301)

"أنا بنت لله، أرسلني هنا . . . أعطاني بيتاً أرضياً وأسرة عزيزة."
الترنيمة رقم ٤٢

The minute each of us is born we gain an identity. We are born in a specific nation and belong to that nation and thus gain a nationality. It was different for me.

I was born in Jerusalem, in a country that essentially ceased to exist only four years prior to my birth. In 1967, after the Six-Day War, Israel occupied all of my country, including the West Bank and Gaza. The following map shows the change that has happened to Palestine. The dark area shows areas allocated to Palestinians and how it has decreased over the years. After 1995, travel restrictions increased gradually, and the area allotted to Palestinians continued to decrease. It now consists of eight percent of the original land of Palestine.

The four years after 1967 changed many things in the lives of my family and other Palestinians. These changes included a sudden loss of identity because Palestine was not recognized as a country anymore. Palestinians were not allowed to fly their flag. The joy I felt when I saw my Palestinian flag raised up high often lasted only a few hours. The

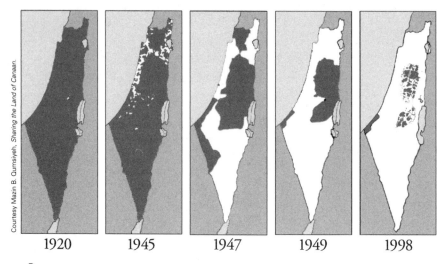

Courtesy Mazin B. Qumsiyeh. *Sharing the Land of Canaan.*

1920   1945   1947   1949   1998

Shutterstock/railwayfx

Palestinian flag.

Israeli soldiers would quickly spot the flag and force a Palestinian, at gunpoint, to take it down and burn it. I felt a part of me die each time I watched my beloved flag burn.

Israeli police and soldiers were now in charge. Even with birth registration, my father had to stand in line and deal with Israeli officials. Both of my parents had birth certificates issued by the government of Palestine because they were both born before 1948, when the State of Israel was established. My birth certificate, however, was issued by Israel.

My father and mother held Jordanian passports. Neither of them was Jordanian, but it was the only passport they were allowed to have at the time. When we needed to leave our country for any reason, we had to obtain a special permit issued by the State of Israel. I remember the first time I planned to leave Palestine was to visit my sister Samar, who then lived in Jordan. I was so excited to travel and see my sister.

*My mother's birth certificate, issued by the government
of Palestine, in English, Arabic, and Hebrew.*

I stood in long lines with other Palestinians trying to get permission from Israeli government officials to leave the country. We would apply at the Israeli civil administration building in Bethlehem. Many people gathered at the door, begging an Israeli soldier to let them in. The soldier said he wouldn't let them in unless they formed a line. But, since everyone had been waiting there for so long, they all wanted to be at the front of the line. No one would choose to go to the back of the line. I did not try to shove my way to the front because I did not want to be squeezed between strange men, so I waited at the end of the line. The soldier again told everyone to line up, but again there was no response. I waited and hoped that somehow we would be allowed in. After hours of waiting, I went home at the end of the day and decided to come back and try again the next day.

In most cases, Palestinians were denied the right to travel. I, however, was hopeful, since I was seventeen years old at the time and I saw no reason why my permit would be denied. Our ten-hour wait finally ended when my name was called. But our relief soon turned to shock when we were told that my petition to leave the country was denied. My father, upset and frustrated, demanded to speak to the Israeli commanding officer. We waited two more hours until my father was allowed to meet with him. I waited outside in the hall. I was tired and hungry after the long hours of waiting. As my father walked out of the office, I expected signs of relief, but his face showed discouragement and anger. I asked him what had happened, and he said that the Israeli commanding officer had said that I was denied the exit permit because I was "a troublemaker." That sounded preposterous to me! I was a seventeen-year-old girl who was uninformed of the political turmoil and complexities around me.

When I was finally granted permission to leave the country a few months later, I learned what my people had to endure in order to cross the bridge between Israel and Jordan. Israeli soldiers emptied my bags on the counter and searched every item, even my underwear. But the worst part was the body search. I had heard about body searches and had dreaded it happening to me. I tried to let my brain wander to make me less aware of what was about to happen. I dragged my feet toward the large pile of shoes on the bridge, placed my shoes there, and then proceeded to the booth, doubly concerned because I was on my period. I knew that I had to remove all my clothes, and I was very shy about my body as a seventeen-year-old. I did not want to take off my underwear. I walked into the booth, and a young female Israeli soldier entered. She seemed to be only slightly older than I was. Her brown military uniform covered her body, and a large M-16 rifle hung on her shoulder. In broken Arabic she demanded, "*Ishlakh kullu*" ("Take everything off").

I slowly proceeded to take off my pants, my shirt, my undershirt. . . . I stopped with only my underwear on, staring at the soldier. My eyes were silently begging, "Please don't make me take this off!" For some reason, she was merciful to me. After she searched my nearly naked body, I sighed in relief when she demanded that I put my clothes on again.

Shortly after that trip to Jordan, I planned to travel to the United States for the first time to stay with my brother Mazin and his wife. This time, I had to obtain not only a travel permit but also a travel document. Since I didn't have a nationality that was recognized by the United States, I traveled using an Israeli travel document. I entered the United States not sure what to expect. I walked slowly toward the immigration officer, who asked me for my papers. I handed him an Israeli travel document and a Jordanian passport.

The officer, probably a bit confused, asked me, "What is your nationality?" I stared at him speechless, unsure what answer to give. Could I tell him I was Palestinian? I possessed no document to support that claim. I am not Jordanian. I am not Israeli. So I chose to remain quiet.

The officer, thinking that I had not understood his question, repeated it: "Ma'am, what—is—your—nationality?"

Still unsure whether my answer would be valid, I answered, "I am Palestinian."

He looked at me and then at my documents, confused. A moment later, he nodded. "Oh, I see, West Bank."

Growing up, I longed for that identity. I wanted to have a passport—a Palestinian one. I wanted to have a country I could call my own, where I could be treated with dignity and respect. I needed to feel a sense of belonging somewhere. Because of the restrictions imposed on us by the occupation, sometimes I felt like a stranger even in my own country.

One year I was in the United States when my American friends around me celebrated their Independence Day. I joined them to watch a parade through town and then watch the fireworks afterward. I closed my eyes and tried to imagine what it would feel like to have this day be a celebration of our independence—the establishment of a Palestinian state. I tried to think of how I would feel if the flags that were raised were Palestinian flags instead of American flags; if the colors that filled the area were not red, white, and blue but black, red, green, and white. I tried to get a taste of the joy people around me felt as they celebrated their country's independence. I watched the fireworks with eyes full of tears as I came to realize that I would never know how that felt. I so wanted to stop people around me and ask them, "How do you feel? What does it feel like to be free? What does it feel like to have an identity and a nationality and be called 'American'?"

Since then, I have come to realize that these titles and identities that the world uses are not as important as some may think. I have come to realize my true identity. I've discovered that this identity is not something the occupation can take away, nor is it something that others can burn or destroy. I speak of my identity as a daughter of God. I didn't need a paper document to prove the sacred relationship I had with God. I was part of God's kingdom, a kingdom with a perfectly just King, even the Lord and Savior Jesus Christ. No occupation, no army, and no weapon in the world could take that away from me. My Palestinian identity has become secondary to me. As long as I know that I am a daughter of the most majestic Being in existence, nothing else matters.

Paul reminds us of this, saying, "The Spirit itself beareth witness with our spirit, that we are the children of God: and if children, then heirs; heirs of God, and joint-heirs with Christ; if so be that we suffer with him, that we may be also glorified together" (Romans 8:16–17).

One day as I was coming home from Jerusalem, I glimpsed some Palestinian men who had been caught by Israeli soldiers during an attempt to sneak into Jerusalem. The men were made to stand and face the wall, which only added to their humiliation. As I passed by them, all of a sudden an enormous feeling surged within me. I sensed how much Heavenly Father loves those men. They matter to Him because they are His children. No matter what others do to humiliate and demoralize us in this imperfect world, we never lose our worth as children of God.

President Uchtdorf said: "Think of the purest, most all-consuming love you can imagine. Now multiply that love by an infinite amount—that is the measure of God's love for you. God does not look on the outward appearance. I believe that He doesn't care one bit if we live in a castle or a cottage, if we are handsome or homely, if we are famous or forgotten. Though we are incomplete, God loves us completely. Though we are imperfect, He loves us perfectly. Though we may feel lost and without compass, God's love encompasses us completely" ("The Love of God," *Ensign*, Nov. 2009, 22).

My contentment and joy in life are not dependent on chains, walls, fences, or checkpoints. As long as I know that I have a Father in Heaven that loves me and cares about me, all is well. In His sight, I am precious. There is no reason to care about what others think of me. As long as I know that I am walking in His paths and obeying His commandments, I know that my Heavenly Father will be there to lift me and help me.

This knowledge that I have gained about my true identity has been life changing to me. However, this knowledge came later in my life. Before I came to understand this, before discovering my true identity, I was engulfed in misery.

Chapter 3

DESPAIR

*"We literally cannot despair—unless we choose to. . . . We can
choose to feed the darkness and death in our lives, or we can choose
to feed the brightness of hope in our lives."—Chieko N. Okazaki*

"لا نستطيع الشعور باليأس إلا إن نحن رغبنا ذلك. بإمكاننا أن نختار
بين تغذية الظلام والموت في حياتنا، أو تغذية الأمل الذي يسطع بنوره
المشرق في حياتنا." تشييكو ن. اوغازاكي

My rebellious, teenage mind struggled to understand the chaos and
tension that surrounded me and Palestinians in general. When I
graduated from high school in 1987, the Intifada (the term Palestinians
use for "uprising") started. Young Palestinians went into the streets to
protest against the Israeli occupation. They asked for their right to have a
nationality, freedom to travel, the ability to raise their flag, and the right
to live in dignity. Young men and boys blocked roads with piles of rocks
and burned tires to show their frustrations and indicate to the Israeli
soldiers that there was a protest. When the Israeli soldiers came into view,
sometimes the young men threw stones at them, leading to their protest
being called *Intifadat Al Hijara*, the "Stone Uprising." During this first
uprising (1987–1993), soldiers responded to such demonstrations by firing tear gas bombs and rubber or plastic bullets at the stone-throwers. A
"rubber" bullet is a misnomer in that these projectiles are actually metal

bullets with a thin rubber or plastic coating. Soldiers used live ammunition at times, but not extensively, during the first uprising. Many areas of Palestine reported deaths of Palestinian stone-throwers, including some young men in my hometown.

Anton was one of those young men. He was attending Bethlehem University at the same time I was, and he was my cousin's classmate at the university. Anton was killed by rubber bullets that were shot into his body by an Israeli soldier. A magazine report describes what happened:

"As Anton left a steep path that ran down into a street leading to his house, he was stopped by the two border policemen and shoved against the wall of a neighboring house with his hands raised. Two women eyewitnesses, one at her door a few yards away and another on a balcony across the street, saw one of the policemen thrust his automatic weapon into the young man's back and fire three rounds of rubber bullets into Anton's body. The Makassed Hospital report . . . described extensive injuries causing massive internal bleeding, the blood eventually flooding the lungs. X-rays revealed square-shaped bullets in Anton's body, the rubber thinly coating their metal cores.

"Seizing Anton, who weighed only about 130 pounds, the Israeli border policemen dragged him down a flight of stone steps to a concealed balcony adjoining the house below. Without calling for an ambulance or medical help they then disappeared, leaving him bleeding to death. Later a small private car took Anton to Jerusalem, where doctors struggled in vain to save his life." (*Washington Report on Middle East Affairs*, July 1992, 38, 87)

After Anton was killed, we walked in a demonstration protesting his murder. The soldiers came and shot tear gas bombs toward us. I had smelled tear gas so often by that point that I was almost immune to its effects. My nose and throat hurt because the tear gas bombs were close, but I was able to withstand their effect. However, during the demonstration, the gas made a young man fall beside me and start shaking on the road. I stood frozen, unsure how to help him. The only thing I could think to do was kick the tear gas bomb away, lessening its effect.

I went to other demonstrations and every time someone was shot or killed, I wished it had been me. I envied those who were killed, because at that time in my life I wished to die. Everyone seemed to be depressed—especially my mother, who was fixed in front of the television watching what was going on all over the country. Young Palestinian men who demonstrated were arrested or shot at, and some had their homes demolished by Israeli bulldozers. People were losing their livelihoods as businesses and schools were closing. We were under curfew often. During curfew we weren't allowed to leave our homes for days or sometimes weeks. As my mother observed these difficulties, she would often remark, "Why would God allow this to happen? If there is a God, why does He not stop these injustices?"

Many Palestinians I know have struggled with their faith in God as a result of the atrocities we have experienced. My maternal grandfather, Issa, lost his faith when he was a child. He felt God had abandoned him. Consequently, he insisted that his children have no religion. On my mother's birth certificate, he made sure it said "none" for religion. However, my grandmother, Milia, had strong faith and attended church regularly with her children. Because of Milia's devotion, my mother grew up having strong faith in God. My mother's faith kept her alive when she was near death right after I was born. That strong faith seemed to wither as the situation in my country worsened. I didn't know how to respond to my mom's questions. In fact, I started to wonder the same things myself: *Does God hate the Palestinians? If not, why would He let us suffer like that?*

At the time when the first uprising started, I was not interested in politics, so I kept myself distant from these demonstrations. However, what happened on October 29, 1987, changed all that. The events of that day are forever engraved in my mind.

I began attending Bethlehem University that fall. I was sixteen years old and oblivious to the various political ideologies around me. The day began with me attending my classes just like any other day. It was late morning when some of my fellow students organized a demonstration on campus. Students carried protest signs and shouted against the Israeli occupation. Some of them gathered rocks to throw at the Israeli soldiers when they arrived. I remember a friend of mine gathering stones, and I asked her what she was going to do with them. I remember being so surprised because she was a woman, and I didn't think women threw stones like the men did. But she said she was collecting them to give to the male students.

The university gates were closed to prevent direct clashes and serious injuries to the students. Bethlehem University is surrounded by a ten-foot wall, making it difficult to get in and out when the gate is closed. A few students inside the walls threw stones at the soldiers stationed outside the walls. In return, the soldiers fired tear gas bombs at those students. Along with many other students, I waited inside one of the buildings instead of participating. We could still smell tear gas, especially downstairs in the physics department, but it was bearable. Because going out into the open was not possible, we stayed in the science faculty building, which also housed a small university clinic.

With a university of only 2,000 students, the clinic was not equipped to handle a large number of patients or serious injuries. However, shortly after the exchange with the soldiers began, we saw students being carried into the clinic. At first their injuries were related to the tear gas. Some had passed out, and others were very dizzy. But then we noted students with bullet wounds being admitted. Due to the lack of space in the clinic, students who had passed out after inhaling tear gas were taken to the science lecture hall, and those with gunshot wounds were taken to the clinic. The clinic was not equipped with personnel or supplies to do much other than stop the bleeding. We watched as more injured students were carried into the clinic. Blood dripped on the floors of our science department. I told my friend that I could not take the sight of blood and wanted to go outside to get a breath of fresh air (what was I thinking?). A few other students joined us as we walked outside and ran behind the building, because the tear gas smell was most severe closer to the main door.

Even when hiding behind the building, we could smell the tear gas. The pain it caused in my throat and nose, however, was a small price to pay to avoid the horrible sight inside. But the painful smell increased, and I soon regretted my decision to go outside. The soldiers continued to fire tear gas bombs near the door, so we could not return inside. Suddenly, the world around me started to spin, and I felt I was about to faint. The tear gas smell was so strong that my friends and I began to lose consciousness. It was at that moment that I realized that my bad decision could have serious consequences.

As I was about to fall to the ground, I caught a glimpse of a hand holding a slice of onion under my nose. "Here, smell this," a voice said. Were it not for the stranger with the onions, we would have passed out. Onion works well to stop the effect of tear gas. Our rescuer told us to put the onion by our nose and run for the door. We were happy to make it back inside, where the smell of tear gas was not as strong. As you may have guessed, we did not dare go outside again.

We waited inside for what felt like days, although it was only several hours. The soldiers would not allow anyone to leave the university, so we had to stay inside and wait. A few hours later we saw people bring in another injured student, Isaac. Two people were holding his legs and two others were holding his arms as they rushed him to the clinic. The hallway was silent, and all eyes were fixed on that student with the dark complexion who seemed, unlike the others who had been brought in, not to be moving.

This injury was different, and everyone knew it. Isaac's wound was in his head, and the clinic personnel could do nothing to help him. We heard that Isaac had been on the roof of the cafeteria hanging a Palestinian flag when an Israeli soldier shot him in the head. We all waited with anticipation—we expected Isaac to be rushed to a hospital. But he was not. The soldiers would not allow him or anyone else to leave the campus. We sat there for two hours as Isaac fought for his life. Everyone was silent. Suddenly nothing else mattered. Isaac was slowly dying.

The mayor of Bethlehem spoke to the soldiers, and they finally allowed Isaac to be taken to a hospital. The doctor rolled him away down the hallway as we all lined up on either side. Isaac looked as if he were asleep, even smiling, from one side of his face, but from the other side, where the large hole in his head was visible, he looked dead. After Isaac was rolled away, the students in unison started singing patriotic songs. I felt power and consolation in the words to one of the songs: "It is all right if we die, if we will root out death from our land."

What happened at the university that day changed my life forever. Isaac, who was the oldest child in his family, was a senior majoring in English literature. His parents had been unable to find work and were anxiously awaiting Isaac's graduation so he could work to support the family. When soldiers took Isaac away from the hospital in Bethlehem only a short time after he was admitted, we did not know whether he was alive or dead. We later learned that his body was taken to an Israeli hospital, where many of his organs were transplanted into Israeli patients. At midnight, soldiers brought Isaac's lifeless and empty body to his home in the Aida Refugee Camp and allowed only his parents to accompany their transport of the body to a remote field far from Bethlehem. We heard that soldiers dug a hole and threw Isaac's body inside and then covered the hole with rocks and dirt. I can't imagine how Isaac's parents felt that night as they saw their beloved son's body being desecrated so horribly.

By Israeli military order, Bethlehem University was closed following the events of that day and remained closed for two years. For a long time afterward, I sat in my room contemplating what had happened. I tried to understand why the Israeli soldiers would do something like that. What they did to Isaac seemed inhuman. I allowed hate and anger to linger in my heart. With that came more frustration, sadness, and rebellion.

I started participating in demonstrations. I did not throw rocks but went out on marches, carrying signs with slogans against the occupation. In an attempt to stop the increasing demonstrations, the military enforced frequent curfews. Because leaving our homes and going to the market for food was forbidden while under curfew and because many curfews lasted for several days, we began growing vegetable gardens and raising animals behind our homes to sustain ourselves. To avoid being seen by the soldiers, we watered the garden and cared for the animals at night, since even going out to the garden was forbidden during curfew. Some got shot simply for looking out of the window. As a consequence of those frequent curfews, schools, universities, and most businesses closed.

Education is very important to the Palestinian people. The majority of Palestinians are educated. The occupation has taken nearly everything from us, but we feel education is the one thing that can't be taken away. It's especially important because without education, we have no chance to obtain work. Since the opening of new factories or certain businesses is often forbidden by the Israeli authorities, the job market for Palestinians is pretty slim. Without a college degree, or often even a post-graduate degree, many stand no chance of finding work. The occupation has taken away our identity, but if we excel in the pursuit of knowledge, we feel that we regain it. Obtaining jobs in high positions can increase our influence and may alter the future.

Everyone goes to school, and public schools are, for the most part, free of charge. We had six years of elementary school, where English is now taught starting in the first grade. Then there are three years of preparatory school (the equivalent of junior high in the USA) and three years of secondary school (the equivalent of high school in the USA). After completing the last year of secondary school, there is a standard exam, called the *Tawjihi,* upon which entry to universities is based. The exam is comprehensive and involves several subjects, including chemistry, physics, mathematics, biology, Arabic and English literature, and social studies. On the first-semester exam, I earned a score of 87.8%, and that was the lowest score I'd ever received in my life. The last year of high school I moved to a new school and had a hard time adjusting, which may have been why I did poorly on the exam. I cried my eyes out. The second semester I scored 93.6%, raising my average to 90.7%. I still was not happy with that, but it was a lot better than the 87.8% I had initially received. My classmates would study all day, every day for these exams. I had one classmate who told me that she had slept only four hours each night and did not leave her room during the entire two weeks that the exams were administered. My cousin Rana and I, however, rarely studied and still did well, even considering that my brother-in-law, who was also our physics teacher, was detained right before we took the second exam.

During the first uprising, government-imposed curfews mandated that schools be closed as a form of punishment against Palestinians. So we started what we called "neighborhood schools." Relocating school to one of our homes, adults gathered neighborhood children, and volunteers from the area assumed the roles of teachers. I taught at one of those neighborhood schools to help Palestinian children take their minds off the terror going on around them and to help them learn.

The Bethlehem economy was heavily dependent on tourism, and fewer tourists in the country created a financial crisis. Most of the olivewood carvings that are sold to tourists are made in my town of Beit Sahour. I have many family members who make their living by selling these amazing olivewood carvings to tourists. The bad political and economic situation caused some people from my town and from other cities in Palestine to leave the country in order to seek employment and a better life for themselves and their children. Many who left were Christians, and the Christian population in Bethlehem decreased gradually. When my mother was in school, her class had one Muslim girl and the rest were Christians. When I went to school, there were maybe five Muslim girls in my class. Now, if you go to an elementary public school in Palestine, you will find the majority of the students to be Muslim. Muslims and Christians in Palestine typically live in absolute harmony. I had and still have many friends who are Muslim. They are good people, generous and devoted to their faith and to God. Sadly, the image of Muslims these days is being stained by the terrorist acts of extremists.

Since Bethlehem University was now closed, I did not have much to do with my time except think about the situation I was in. As I watched people in my town get arrested or beaten or shot, I wondered why God had abandoned me and my people. Making matters worse, the international media depicted the Palestinians as the "bad guys," as if it was a crime to fight for our freedom and human rights.

Aside from the occasional demonstrations, I sat in my room and

Demonstration in Beit Sahour after a Palestinian was killed in 2000.

thought about my situation. It seemed hopeless. My university was closed, as were all the other Palestinian universities. I witnessed the mothers of martyrs crying and saw the suffering of the people whose children were arrested or whose houses were demolished, and my heart ached. I felt my heart fill with the darkness of anger and hate. I longed to die. In fact, during some demonstrations, everyone else ran from the Israeli soldiers while I stood still. I thought death was the only way to end my misery, because I saw no hope in the future. I began to pray to Heavenly Father, asking Him to end my life. One day I prayed with such intensity and faith that I thought He must have heard me.

A Day in My Life 2

Background: A journal entry from a cold Sabbath day in January. I tried to go to church after a bombing in Jerusalem, which added a few extra challenges to my weekly trip there.

Two days ago there was a bombing in Jerusalem. A man from Bethlehem (twenty-four years old) went into an Israeli bus and blew himself up, along with the rest of the Israelis on the bus. Some may question, what would cause a person to kill himself like that? As we heard the news, a girl that sat next to me in the taxi proceeded to explain why someone would want to do that. She said her brother did the same thing because he let his anger and desire for revenge drive him. She explained that her brother watched the Israeli soldiers shoot and kill both his father and his uncle. Therefore, he wanted revenge and wanted to end his own life. She said that most of those who commit these suicide bombings have been beaten or arrested and tortured by the Israeli soldiers. Some of them had their houses demolished, and some of them were shot or watched someone they knew get shot.

After the bombing that day in Jerusalem, people in my town expected an Israeli invasion of Bethlehem. They expected long days of curfew, and so everyone bought so much food to store in case they needed it. At 4:00 a.m. on Friday, we were woken up by the sounds of the Israeli tanks and helicopters going into the Bethlehem area from all directions. Curfew was imposed on the Aida refugee camp (which is where the man was from) and nearby areas. The soldiers demolished the house of the man who blew himself up and arrested many people from the Aida refugee camp. Checkpoints were placed on all roads exiting the city, and no one was allowed in or out of the Bethlehem area.

Today, Saturday, I planned to go to church at the Jerusalem Center. The taxi drivers said all the roads are closed and it was impossible to leave. They said that even Palestinians with a valid permit were turned back. There was a checkpoint at the edge of my town. Even people who lived on the other side of the checkpoint were not allowed to go to their houses and had to stay with friends in town. To get to Jerusalem, I would have to cross that checkpoint and two others as well. The taxi driver took us on a long detour. It took us an hour to get around that first checkpoint. When we got to the second checkpoint, the taxi driver told us he did not want to get close to the soldiers. He said the soldiers broke the glass of the taxis that were within 100 meters of the checkpoint. He also said that the soldiers would not allow anyone to go through the checkpoint. I got off the taxi and started going up the hill to go around the checkpoint; everyone did. I saw old people, children, and even women who had groceries they were taking to Jerusalem to sell; they all went up the hill. I helped one of the women carry her bag since she was really out of breath. She paid for my taxi in order to return my favor. I found another taxi at the top of the hill, and it took us to Abu Dis. From there, we took another taxi to the "gate." This gate is the only opening in the separation wall that leads to Jerusalem. When I got to the gate, I discovered that there were Israeli soldiers at the gate, so I would not be able to cross to Jerusalem. We turned around and the taxi took us to a place called "in between the walls." I walked for a while on a muddy road until I got to the main road, where I waited for a taxi or bus. A taxi came and immediately asked, "Jerusalem identity card, or West Bank?" When I told him I did not have a Jerusalem identity card, he said he could take me only a few blocks, then I would have to get off. I agreed and got on the taxi. He took me only as far as Al-Maqased hospital on the Mount of Olives (this is where I was born). From there I walked to the Jerusalem Center. I made it there a few minutes before church started.

We had a great meeting at church. I got to teach Sunday School and I enjoyed doing that. Shortly after, I had to be back on the road again. Leaving Jerusalem is much easier than getting into Jerusalem. There is a bus that goes directly from Jerusalem to Beit Jala, which is next to Bethlehem. This time, however, the bus reached Beit Jala to find a checkpoint at the entrance. The soldiers checked our identity cards to make sure that they were Bethlehem identity cards before they let us through.

People from other towns were not allowed in. After we were checked, we noticed the soldier next to the bus fire a shot from his rifle into the air. Then he aimed at a small white car in the road and started shooting. Apparently the soldier had ordered the driver in the white car to stop, and the driver did not hear him. I watched the car, hoping the driver and those inside were all right. I was happy to see them get off the car unharmed. They all immediately lifted their shirts, revealing their bare skin, and put their arms up in the air. This was a standard search procedure when you were stopped by soldiers like that. The sound of the shots was so loud; I had never been this close to a firing rifle. The woman next to me said she sees this all the time and it is normal for her.

Fifty meters from that checkpoint was a place called "Al-sider." This is simply a pile of dirt that the soldiers had put up to close the road leading out of Beit Jala. I climbed over the pile of dirt and was met by another group of soldiers who again asked for my identity card. The woman that was sitting next to me in the bus said she was glad that the invasion did not involve curfew in her area and that it was just road closures. I am amazed how the people here find reasons to be grateful among everything that is going on.

Chapter 4

LEGACY

"It is good to look to the past to gain appreciation for the present and perspective for the future. It is good to look upon the virtues of those who have gone before, to gain strength for whatever lies ahead."—Gordon B. Hinckley

"من المفيد أن ننظر تجاه الماضي كي نستطيع أن نُقدّر قيمة الحاضر ونتطلّع للمستقبل. من المفيد أن ننظر إلى حسنات من سبقونا كي نكسب القوة التي تساعدنا على المَضي قُدماً." غوردون ب. هنكلي

One morning in 1988, I arose and began bidding farewell to everything around me. I said goodbye to the flowers, to the trees, to my family, and to life as I knew it. At only seventeen, I felt I would soon die. I was not sad but in fact felt quite relieved and happy. The reason was simple: I had prayed to God the night before to end my life, and this time I sensed that my prayer would be answered. Unlike previous times, this time I had prayed with faith and intensity. But then that day, to my surprise, concluded as every other had; I was still alive. I waited and waited for God to answer my prayer, but the answer didn't come. So I began to think proactively, imagining ways to end my own life, but without the courage to carry out my plans. The easiest way, I decided, was to become a suicide bomber. But I didn't want to kill anyone in the explosion—that is, no one except me.

However, I could not do it. After all, I was not a quitter. Instilled in me was the strength to persevere and stay strong. I come from a long line of people who had fought to live and to survive, against all odds. My desire to end it all, to give in, was a sign of despair so deep that it almost had the power to reach up and grab me by my throat. But I didn't kill myself—maybe because of the legacy of perseverance, of fighting for life, that ran too strong in the blood I carried in my veins.

An example of that is my grandfather, Issa Atallah. His story shows how one poor boy who lost his whole family and belongings during the war could persevere and succeed in life. Issa had every reason to give up, but he worked hard and kept on moving.

I begin my grandfather's story when he was five years old. He was playing in the street with his friends when he overheard people say that the "drums of war" were heard in Bethlehem. Issa recalled that drums were instruments played at weddings and joyous occasions. So he did

not anticipate that this specific drum sound would change his life forever. He did not foresee that this "war drum" would be the beginning of long years of misery for him and result in the loss of all his family members.

Named Issa (*Jesus*) by his father after the babe born in Bethlehem, my grandfather was born to Mariam (*Mary*) and Atallah (*God's gift*) in 1908 in Beit Sahour, Palestine. When the drums of war sounded, Atallah made a good living running a factory that carved

Issa Atallah (my maternal grandfather).

43

the mother of pearl and beads used in rosaries that were sold to the tourists in Bethlehem.

In reality, the "drum" marked the start of the First World War. Issa's difficult journey began when his father was required to serve in the Turkish army, leaving Mariam to care for Issa and his younger siblings Mitry, Ilias, and Hilwa. Atallah went to Jerusalem and from there traveled to Syria as part of his military duty. The factory owned by Atallah closed, since all the workers were also sent to fight, thus ending the only source of income for the family.

Issa tasted hunger for the first time in his life. At his young age of five, he would roam the dusty streets of Beit Sahour searching for food. "Look!" Issa joyfully told his cousin one day as he grasped the orange peel that he had dug out of the trash. He held the peel in his hand as if it were a diamond. Issa had a large smile on his face as he shoved the orange peel in his mouth and swallowed it. The taste of the orange peel was much sweeter than the bitter weeds and grass he had had for dinner the day before.

The agony of watching her starving children was too difficult for Issa's mother to bear. As soon as she heard that conditions were better in Jordan, Mariam immediately took Issa and the rest of her children there. With her four children, all under six years old, she walked from Beit Sahour to Al-Salt in Jordan, a distance of about sixty miles. After Mariam begged refuge from several families in Al-Salt, one family allowed them to live in a stable designated for animals in the back of their house (the metaphor here is interesting: Mary and Jesus in a stable!).

Desperate and starving, Mariam and her family simply tried to survive day to day. Before long, contaminated water sources brought cholera to the family, and they were asked to leave their stable shelter, as their host family feared the deadly disease would spread to them. Finally settling in a cave near Madaba, the care of the family was left to the oldest and healthiest child, six-year-old Issa.

Issa foraged for scraps of food, begged door-to-door for money or food, and convinced shepherds to give him leftover water after the sheep had drunk from it. Cholera, starvation, and exposure each took their toll. Before long, Mitry and Hilwa died. Issa helped his mother dig graves inside the cave where they lived so that they could bury the sweet little shriveled bodies. Mariam grew sicker and soon realized that sickness and death were all the family would experience if they remained in Jordan. Unable to walk, she resolved to pay a Bedouin man everything they owned if he would take them back to Beit Sahour on his donkey. Issa helped tie his mother, who by then was too sick to even sit up straight, to the back of the Bedouin man's donkey and then strapped baby Ilias behind her. Taking turns holding the baby in place, Issa and the Bedouin slowly trekked the sixty miles back to Beit Sahour.

Somehow, Mariam survived the journey. And as their pitiful group made its way up the streets of Beit Sahour, the exhausted Issa looked up to see his father rushing toward them. Atallah had deserted the army and returned home, only to find his family gone. Now, overjoyed with relief at their reappearance, he rushed toward them, pulling Mariam from the donkey. Cradling his decimated family in his arms, Atallah looked helplessly into the eyes of his wife, who uttered only one final, exhausted word—"Atallah"—before breathing her last breath on the dusty streets of Beit Sahour.

After losing many battles, the Turkish authorities started to find and arrest those who had fled military service. Among those arrested was Atallah, who was sent to Damascas and then to Tiberias (Galilee), leaving little Issa and Ilias behind. The only relative willing to take in the two boys was a blind aunt who was barely able to support herself. Suffering from hunger again, Issa found no alternative but to knock on doors and beg.

After the victory of the British army and the withdrawal of the Turks and Germans from most towns, Atallah escaped from the defeated Turkish army. No longer afraid of arrest and punishment, he reopened his souvenir workshop and started also working as a barber. Stability briefly returned to the broken family. Finding it difficult to take care of two young boys on his own, Atallah decided to remarry. A few days before the wedding, however, he had severe pains in his right side. The only doctor available at that time was the "Roman doctor," who was actually a Greek doctor who went around on his white donkey. This doctor's way of treating patients was to look into their mouths and then give them a prescription consisting of English salt or castor oil. When the pain did not subside, Atallah sought further medical help from a French doctor at the Tantur Convent north of Bethlehem. This doctor advised putting some hot pads on the site of the pain. Atallah's appendix, exceedingly swollen at that point, quickly exploded as a result of the heat. He died the very next day, a fall day in 1918. Adding to the tragedy, within a few weeks, Ilias, who never regained his full strength after being ill, also died. Issa, now barely ten years old, found himself alone in the world. Betrayed by his extended family, Issa vowed that he would use only his father's name, Atallah, as his last name.

The war had ended and many rejoiced, but for Palestinians it was a sad ending. At the end of the war, Arthur Balfour, the British Foreign Secretary, indicated Britain's support of the establishment of a Jewish state in the land of Palestine. Although unforeseen at that time, over the years, the Zionist movement would work toward an all-Jewish state in Palestine, making life for the Palestinians who already lived there very difficult.

Now that the war was over, Issa, a smart and ambitious boy, was determined not to be poor anymore. He wanted to go to school, believing education would be his only ticket out of his misery. One day as he was walking toward a field, he met his cousin Michael Qumsiyeh. Michael told Issa about a school he was attending in Jerusalem called Schneller. It was a school for orphaned Palestinian children, known as the Syrian Orphan House. Michael told Issa how wonderful the school was and that it offered great food and shelter. Issa desired to go to that school with all his heart.

When the summer break was over and Michael prepared to head back to his school, Issa begged his cousin to take him along. Michael agreed, so the two young boys headed on foot to Jerusalem, about five miles from Beit Sahour. They reached the school right before sunset. Issa was so excited at the thought of going to school that he hardly noticed how tired he was and how sore his bare feet were. Reaching the gate of the school, Michael alone was allowed in—because he wore the school uniform—but Issa was denied entry. Issa's attire that day was a robe crudely made from army tent fabric, the only thing he had managed to find to cover his thin body. The boys begged and pleaded with the guard to let Issa in, but the guard wouldn't even allow him to spend the night at the school. Without knowing the way home by himself, Issa crumpled to the ground by the gate in fatigue and fear and began to cry in the darkness. His pathetic plight soon attracted other children, who came to comfort the little boy.

The commotion also caught the attention of Maria Schneller, sister of the school's president, Herman Schneller. When she saw Issa, the focus of all the attention, she was touched by his torn and dirty clothes, bare feet, and tears. Upon hearing Issa's story, Maria called the sewing teacher and told him to give Issa a place to sleep that night and to bring him to her in the morning so she could decide what to do. Issa never forgot that night. He spent it on the ground, outside the front door of the teacher's house, with mice scurrying around him all night.

When the sun rose, Issa was taken to Miss Maria's office near the main entrance of the school. Wanting to do more to help the boy, she sent him to the warehouse so he could take a hot bath. Issa had never before experienced a bath with hot water. He was also given new, clean clothes. Washed and properly attired, Issa was ready to face the principal, Elias Nasrallah Haddad. He evaluated Issa and admitted him to the third grade at Schneller.

One last obstacle stood in Issa's way to begin school: he needed funds to purchase notebooks, pencils, books, clothes, and other necessities. Other orphans had relatives who gave them the money needed for these supplies, but Issa did not have anyone who would help him. He finally located a nice man named Tuma, who offered Issa a loan that would cover what he needed for school. Issa worked after school and during holidays repairing shoes so he could pay off his loan. Recognizing his remarkable good fortune, Issa worked hard in school to prove he was worth the help he had been given. Within only a few weeks, he moved up two grades, to the fifth grade, due to his diligence and aptitude. After sixth grade, he was ready to start an apprenticeship to prepare for his life's profession. Mr. Haddad, the principal, offered him a job working in the government warehouses in Jerusalem. Issa made three pounds a month. He kept only twenty-five pennies for his personal allowance and gave the rest to the school for his room and board.

In the little spare time he had, Issa read as many books as possible. He soon heard of a school in Jerusalem called the Teachers' Training College. He was told that those who completed the sixth grade successfully were invited to attend this school for three years. Upon graduation from the Teachers' Training College, he would be eligible to teach elementary school. Issa passed the required proficiency exam but learned during the interview that incoming students needed to be at least fifteen years old to be admitted. Issa, who was only fourteen at the time, was invited to apply again the following year. So he went back home to Beit Sahour and continued earning money by repairing shoes. He became so well known in his town for his good work and integrity that later, customers waited for him to return from Jerusalem on weekends and holidays to fix their shoes. They trusted only him with their shoes!

The next year Issa was accepted at the Teachers' Training College. He graduated in 1927 and began teaching at the Beit Jala Elementary Boy's School near Bethlehem. Issa loved Arabic literature and reading. He later wrote the first Arabic grammar books used in Palestinian schools. He also wrote poetry and children's stories, translating some stories from English. His most important work was on Arabic proverbs. He gathered ancient proverbs from all available sources and published them in a book. Issa was a beloved and successful teacher and writer. In recognition of his contributions to education and on recommendation by the Jordanian Ministry of Education, King Hussein awarded him the Medal of Education of the second degree in 1974. Educating himself and teaching others to learn was Issa's reward in life.

Issa and Milia Atallah and their family. From left to right: Bisher, Fawz, Sami, Hayah, Amal (back row); Humam, Milia, Areej, Issa, Sana (front row).

Issa fell in love with a woman who loved learning and teaching just as much as he did. Milia Jubran Matar was born in 1910 in Nazareth. Her early life shared some similarities with that of Issa. She also struggled to survive the war, and her mother also died while she was young, though it happened during the birth of one of Milia's siblings. Her father got remarried to a German woman, known by everyone as Frau Matar. Even Milia didn't know her first name. That marriage led to Milia being able to help provide food for her family during the First World War. The German soldiers would give her food because they were surprised she could speak German. Milia's father, Jubran Matar, and her stepmother came to Beit Sahour in 1925 to reopen the German Lutheran School that had been closed during the war. That school was located right across the street from the school where Issa taught.

Milia was accepted to the Teachers' Training College at the age of thirteen, a young age for admittance. The principal was impressed with how well she could speak English and thus made an exception.

Atallah Al-Yateem/Di'es
(my great-grandfather).

Hanna Jeries Qumsiyeh
(my paternal grandfather).

After graduating, Milia opened the first public school for girls in the Bethlehem District. She taught girls of all ages at her school, because none of the girls had an education at that time. Issa met Milia through his work in education. Milia and Issa fell in love. They married on July 27, 1930. My mother, Fawz Issa Atallah, was born to this amazing couple on June 19, 1932.

The story of my grandparents and their legacy of perseverance continued with my mother, who overcame all the odds and excelled in her education. She attended school in Jerusalem during the Second World War and never missed a day despite the dangers that faced her as she traveled to school every day. She was at the top of her class and became a teacher right after she graduated. After she married, she continued to teach and inspire her students, becoming the first woman in the area to remain working after marriage. When my mother was in her fifties, she attended Bethlehem University and obtained a bachelor's degree in English literature. My brother Maher, who had earned his PhD, was a professor in the Mathematics Department at Bethlehem University at the

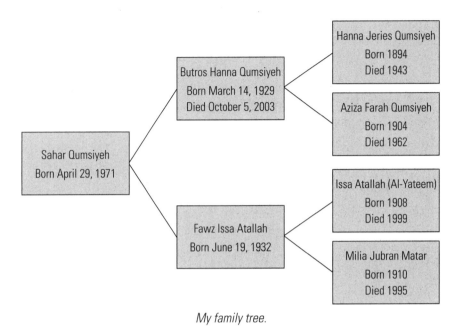

My family tree.

same time that my mother attended. My mother graduated with close to a 4.0 GPA and was probably the best student at the university.

My family taught me that if you work hard for something, you will obtain it. They taught me that if things are hard, persevering and staying strong can help you accomplish your dreams. Things were very hard in my country during the first uprising, but I knew deep down that Heavenly Father was aware of us, even though there was no evidence of that.

I wondered why Heavenly Father didn't answer the prayer to end my life. I went on many marches, and when others would run from the soldiers, I stood still in front of them. Despite my many tries to stand in the line of fire, I survived. I have come to realize that Heavenly Father answers all prayers, but in His own way, not ours. Even that prayer that I uttered in 1988, as crazy as it may seem, was answered. Heavenly Father did end my life; He ended my life of misery, despair, and pain and gave me a new life of light, peace, and happiness in its place.

Chapter 5

TRANSFORMATION

"Yea, behold, I will tell you in your mind and in your heart, by the Holy Ghost, which shall come upon you and which shall dwell in your heart" (D&C 8:2).

"نعم، سوف أعلمك في عقلك وفي قلبك، بواسطة الروح القدس الذي سيحل عليك والذي سيتقر في قلبك." (المبادئ والعهود ٨: ٢)

When Bethlehem University was closed following the death of Isaac, I went to the United States to stay with my brother Mazin. While there, I took some classes at a small community college in Memphis, Tennessee. After being closed for two years, Bethlehem University finally reopened—at least partially. The university had started giving classes in secret, in people's homes and inside some other institutions. So after studying at Shelby State Community College in Memphis for a year, I returned back home to Beit Sahour and started attending Bethlehem University again. I graduated in 1993 with a bachelor's degree in mathematics and started teaching at an elementary school. I soon discovered that teaching elementary school was not something I wanted to do for the rest of my life.

I explored other options that were available to someone with a mathematics degree. My brother Maher suggested that I get a master's degree in statistics. He said that it was a good field and that I could easily find a job after graduation. Because getting a master's degree in my country was not possible, I planned to go to the United States to obtain my degree. However, the salary I made then (about $400 a month) did not enable me to have any savings. There was no way that I could afford to pay for an education in the United States, so I pursued scholarships at several American universities.

I was overjoyed to receive an acceptance and a scholarship to American University in Washington, DC. The scholarship was very generous, totaling $56,000 a year to cover all my schooling and living costs. The thought of leaving the violence, confusion, and hopelessness in Palestine to study in the United States thrilled me.

When I received a phone call soon afterward from a man saying, "Congratulations, you have been granted a scholarship to Brigham Young University," I was understandably silent. *Should I tell him that I am not interested, or should I wait and tell him later?* I thought. Even though I had applied for a BYU scholarship after seeing an ad in the *Al-Quds* local newspaper, I never intended to go to BYU.

The BYU Jerusalem Center is built on Palestinian land. BYU had to lease the land from Israel since the Israeli government does not acknowledge the fact that the land belongs to the Palestinians. In order to pay the Palestinians for using their land, Brigham Young University offers full scholarships to Palestinians. I was being offered one of those scholarships.

My mother mocked me for even applying to BYU, especially since I applied *after* I had received the other scholarship. She said Utah was in the middle of nowhere and was a desert. Because I had never heard of Utah, I thought that my mother might be right and that no one actually lived in Utah. I began making some inquiries and discovered that Mormons, or members of The Church of Jesus Christ of Latter-day Saints, lived in Utah. I had absolutely no idea what Mormons believed, but I had heard rumors from family members and friends about some strange beliefs they held. I later found these reports to be untrue. My grandfather, Issa, shared the sole positive comment I heard about Mormons. He told me that he had met a wonderful Mormon couple who had visited Bethlehem a few years before. He said they were the nicest people he had ever met. During the course of my interview, I also learned that Mormons don't drink tea, coffee, or alcohol. I concluded that Mormons were really strange and doubted I wanted to associate with them.

These random bits of information were my only introduction to the school and its geographic area. So when I received that call from Dr. S. Kent Brown, the director of the Jerusalem Center, congratulating me on my scholarship, I thanked him but had no intention of accepting the offer. I was planning to pursue a graduate degree in Washington, DC. The Jerusalem Center director probably thought he was bringing me great news, but I was already wondering when would be the best time to tell him that I needed to decline the BYU offer.

Later I discovered that the BYU scholarship amounted to only $10,000 a year, less than one-fifth of my scholarship to American University. Of course, part of the reason was the lower cost of living in Utah, but I did not know that at the time. I had a decision to make, though the decision appeared to be easy because it was such an obvious choice. Not surprisingly, everyone I knew advised me to go to Washington, DC. Without warning or explanation, however, I began to feel a yearning in my heart to go to BYU. In the past, I had always relied on others' opinions to determine my decisions. I doubted my own ability to choose wisely. But this decision was different. Deep down, I knew where I needed and wanted to go, and I couldn't allow anyone else to tell me otherwise.

Despite my strong feelings, I struggled with the BYU decision for the longest time. Then, for the first time when faced with making a choice, I decided to ask Heavenly Father for help. Up to this point in my life, my prayers had often been rote, meaningless, and not particularly sincere. I prayed every night, but I said the same set prayer. I would recite, "Our Father who art in heaven. . . ." and then I would ask Him to give me something I wanted. The few occasions when I had prayed from my heart were during the hardest times I had ever experienced—when I had asked Heavenly Father to end my life. I was raised as a Christian and taught to pray, yet I was never taught the way Heavenly Father communicates with us, His children, through the Holy Ghost. So, even though I asked Heavenly Father for guidance about my desire to go to school at BYU, I had no idea how He would answer. After this particular prayer, however, I had this strong feeling in my heart—a feeling I could not deny—saying that I should go to BYU. I did not identify that feeling as coming from the Holy Ghost, but I simply could not shake it. Because the sensation was so strong, my desire to go to BYU only intensified. Yet I still thought that Heavenly Father had not answered my petition, when in fact He *had*. Instead of the strong feeling of assurance, I anticipated a more tangible or even audible answer. Notwithstanding, I followed my feelings and committed to pursue my graduate degree in statistics at BYU.

In the summer of 1994, I filled two big suitcases with all my clothes and took off for Utah. I did not know what to expect. From the little I knew about Mormons, I figured it would be hard to get used to being around them. The strange thing was that from the moment I arrived on BYU's campus, I felt loved and welcomed. Everyone was so nice and friendly to me; the whole environment differed from all the unrest to which I was accustomed back home in Palestine. I found that tears often filled my eyes when someone did something nice for me. Those girls in the dorms will never know how much they touched me with their kindness and acceptance.

It was one thing to feel accepted, however, and quite another thing to imagine changing religions. I never expected to become interested in the LDS Church, if for no other reason than that it was so different from anything I had ever known. It was so new. My roommate invited me to go to church with her, and I did go once or twice. I found the worship service to be interesting but too foreign to me. We met for church at a university classroom, there were no crosses displayed, and the bishop wore regular clothing. Even though I loved everyone on my dorm floor, I felt like a foreigner on Sunday—and most other days. I had come from such a different background and culture. I wanted so much to fit in and feel that I belonged, but that did not happen. My friends talked about dating and shopping and other things that I found so minor in life. My country was under occupation; my people were suffering from violence and loss of freedoms. To me, there was nothing more important than finding peace and safety for my people—certainly not cute guys and the latest fashions. What frustrated me most was that no one around me seemed to know anything about what was happening in my homeland. I tried to explain that my country of Palestine had been occupied by Israel since 1948; that since 1967 my country had no longer existed on the map; that as a people we no longer had a nationality, were forbidden even from displaying our national flag, and were suffering physically and emotionally under the Israeli occupation. But few of my new friends seemed remotely capable of understanding how difficult my life in Palestine was.

During my first year at BYU, I had the chance to listen to part of the general conference of the LDS Church. At first I listened because I was curious about the idea of a prophet speaking. The fact that Mormons called their president a prophet sounded very strange to me. But Mormons believe in continuous revelation and believe that there is a living prophet on the earth, similar to when Moses or Elijah led God's people and received God's will for them. I don't remember much at all of what was said in conference, but I sat up and took note when I heard a speaker refer to my land as "Palestine" rather than calling it "Israel," as most Americans did. This was the first time I had heard any American express what sounded like support for the Palestinians, and I thought a church that did not hate Palestinians must be a good church.

After that session of conference was over, I asked my friend Shae to tell me about her church. Shae told me everything. She started with the Creation of Adam and Eve and the Fall from the Garden of Eden and explained how God has a purpose for our lives in this fallen world. She told me about the plan Heavenly Father has for His children, about the Atonement of Jesus Christ, the Apostasy, and the Restoration of the gospel. I began to understand that our coming here to earth was part of a plan, that we existed as spirits and lived with Heavenly Father before we came to earth. Shae explained our premortal life, our earthly life, and life after death. Others in the room objected to Shae's approach, because they thought she was telling me too much and would confuse me. But to me it was as though Shae were putting all the pieces of a puzzle together, and for the first time I could finally see the beautiful picture—a picture that was so clear and cohesive. I came to understand that life was a test and that the trials and difficulties we face are allowed by a loving Heavenly Father to help us grow and learn to become like Him. It became clear to me that Heavenly Father loves us all, and He loves us perfectly. He *didn't* hate the Palestinians, like I used to think! Everything started to make sense—especially the reason and power of the Atonement of Jesus Christ. Before this, I could not understand why the Savior's death on the cross had any personal meaning. Now, I understood how essential the Atonement was in saving me and everyone else from spiritual and physical death.

Soon after Shae's illuminating explanation, Bryce, a friend of mine from class, gave me a copy of the Book of Mormon that had been translated into Arabic. He told me that the book was named after an ancient prophet who had abridged and combined all the writings of his people into one record. Bryce explained that the book was scripture and contained the words of God, just like the Bible did. He told me that it was also called "another testament of Jesus Christ" because the Book of Mormon provided a second witness to the Bible about the Savior—that He died for us and that He lives today and loves us all.

I began reading the Book of Mormon shortly after receiving it. Bryce advised me to read a small portion of the book and then pray to ask God if the book was true or not, but I decided I would read the whole book first. Because I was taking classes toward my master's degree, I was really busy and did not have as much time to read as I would have liked. However, I started going to LDS Church services, and I learned to love the Church more and more with each visit. Everything that was taught sounded so logical and perfect to my ears and my heart. In the Christian church of my upbringing, I was taught that Heavenly Father, Jesus, and the Holy Ghost were the same being. I can honestly say that this teaching never made any sense to me! Why would the Savior pray to Himself or even speak about the Father if They both were one being? In contrast, it made sense for them to be three separate divine beings, perfectly unified in purpose as taught in The Church of Jesus Christ of Latter-day Saints. I was able to identify the feelings in my heart as the influence of the Holy Ghost, the third member of the Godhead. I had not been aware of the Holy Ghost before or been able to understand His role. Through the Holy Ghost I was able to identify the truthfulness of the things I was learning. I felt the Holy Ghost confirming to me, through a peaceful, sweet feeling in my heart, that I had found the truth.

In the summer of 1995, I finished reading the Book of Mormon. But I never needed to kneel down to ask Heavenly Father if the book was true or if The Church of Jesus Christ of Latter-day Saints was the true church of God. I already knew the answer deep in my heart and with every fiber of my being. Words simply cannot describe my feelings during this time of study and pondering. For the first time in my life, I experienced a sensation of profound peace—peace and remarkable joy. I wrote in my journal, "I didn't think that such peace and joy were possible!"

During that same year that I was discovering truths about the gospel of Jesus Christ, good things were also happening back home in Palestine. Israeli and Palestinian leaders cosigned a treaty called the Oslo Agreement. According to that agreement, Palestinians regained control over some Palestinian cities and were authorized to create the Palestinian Authority. Palestine was still not considered a country, but we were issued Palestinian "passports" (travel documents). Palestine was still not found on any map, meaning it was not recognized as an autonomous nation, but this agreement promised to return some of our rights and freedoms as a people. Under the agreement, Israeli soldiers were not allowed in Palestinian areas, which were under the control of

Courtesy Chad Emmett.

Bethlehem area showing the Separation Wall around the city.

Courtesy Mazin Qumsiyeh.

Har Homa Israeli settlement close to Beit Sahour built on Palestinian land. These illegal settlements house Jews who come to Palestine from various countries.

the Palestinian Authority. For the first time in decades, Palestinians could fly the Palestinian flag in those areas without fearing it would be taken down and burned. These changes meant a lot to us because even though we didn't yet have a country, we again had a place that was finally our own. Police that patrolled Palestinian Authority areas were Palestinians—replacing the Israelis. To me and my fellow Palestinians, the agreement represented a great step, and we were happy to have some independence. But I would soon learn that my optimism was unwarranted, because the terms of the Oslo agreement were not upheld. The Palestinian Authority areas were reduced to contain only a few parts of some major cities surrounded by Israeli walls, checkpoints, and settlements.

A Palestinian passport.

Despite my happiness and joy over learning about Jesus Christ and His gospel, getting baptized and joining the LDS Church never crossed my mind until I witnessed a friend's baptism. The service was wonderful, and as I watched the ordinance being performed, I felt the Holy Ghost confirm to me that baptism should also be my next step. Right after my friend came up out of the water, having been immersed by one with authority from God to perform the ordinance, I knew what I lacked and what I needed to do. I was gradually understanding the role of the Holy Ghost. In the concluding chapter of the Book of Mormon, Moroni exhorts those who read the book to pray and ask God if the Book of Mormon is true. Moroni then promises, "And by the power of the Holy Ghost ye may know the truth of all things" (Moroni 10:5). By following Moroni's promise, I came to understand how the Holy Ghost was guiding and helping me in my life.

After pondering and seeking the Spirit's guidance for days, I decided to join this church that I had come to love. My resolve, however, was suddenly shaken when I began thinking practically. *What would my family say?* I would never know until I shared my new happiness with them. With excitement but also plenty of trepidation, I called my father and mother to tell them that I had decided to be baptized a member of the Church. I don't think I was prepared for their emotional reaction. They were so mad at me that they called me crazy and brainwashed. My mother said that if I did join the Church, I would never marry, everyone would avoid me, and our family's reputation would be ruined. In my hometown of Beit Sahour, everyone knows everyone. I knew the tradition of ostracizing anyone who left their family's religion for a different church. When I thought of the fallout that would occur if I were baptized, my heart broke. *How could I do this to my family?* I felt so good about getting baptized, but to think of how much this decision would hurt my family tore me to pieces. I loved my family, so going against their will would be mean and selfish. I therefore decided to forget about getting baptized. My family and their happiness were more important to me than my personal dreams.

Ignoring or forgetting about the feeling concerning baptism I had received from the Spirit was harder than I would have thought. I continued to go to church—and I came to love it more and more. Soon I could fight my feelings no longer. Regardless of the consequences, I would be baptized. I arranged to be taught by the missionaries. Each investigator receives a series of lessons before qualifying for baptism. For the second lesson, Bryce, my friend who had given me the Book of Mormon, was with me. During the lesson, Bryce asked, "Sahar, are you willing to follow Christ and be baptized?"

I knew he would ask that, and I knew what I would say, but I was still stunned. *Was I really going to do this? Did nothing else matter? Did I really know what kind of commitment I was making?* The answer was yes to all these questions, so I simply said, "Yes."

On February 4, 1996, I was finally baptized. Before it was time to leave my dorm room and go to my baptism, my roommate left me alone to pray. I knelt down and felt an amazing peace and the strongest witness telling me I was doing the right thing. I even opened my eyes to see if the Lord was in the room, because I could feel His presence so strongly. I wish I could explain that feeling of peace to those of you who have never experienced it. I did not want to get up from my knees—I did not want that feeling of peace to leave me. I would soon learn that this was indeed the influence of the Holy Ghost, and I was about to receive an ordinance that would allow Him to be my constant companion.

While growing up in Palestine, I believed in God. I never doubted that He heard my prayers. Yet I believed in a silent God. When Bryce told me to pray to know if the Book of Mormon was true, I was not sure what he meant. Would God answer? Does God speak to people? In those few short months at BYU I learned that God was not silent—that He does speak. He rarely speaks with a loud voice, though; He speaks through a feeling. He speaks through the Holy Ghost with a feeling that penetrates our hearts—a feeling you may be sensing right now as you read this. I had come to realize that Heavenly Father is real and that He cares about me and loves me beyond measure. He answers my every prayer, sometimes not in the way I expect or in the time I want, but He always answers. The way that He answers is perfectly explained in revelations in the Doctrine and Covenants:

"Verily, verily, I say unto you, I will impart unto you of my Spirit, which shall enlighten your mind, which shall fill your soul with joy; and then shall ye know, or by this shall you know, all things whatsoever you desire of me, which are pertaining unto things of righteousness, in faith believing in me that you shall receive" (D&C 11:13–14).

My roommate and I walked to the Joseph Smith Building on BYU campus, where I would be baptized. There were 160 people at my baptism. It was a beautiful service. I still remember walking down into the baptismal font, which was filled with water, with Bryce at my side. I sensed a remarkable feeling when Bryce said the words, "Sahar Qumsiyeh, having been commissioned of Jesus Christ, I baptize you in the name of the Father, and of the Son, and of the Holy Ghost. Amen." Then he lowered me completely under the water. As I came out of the water, I knew that I was born again. Nothing could have made this day more special—except one thing. I longed to have my family there so I could share with them the peace and joy I felt. Because of this covenant that I was making with my Father in Heaven, this amazing feeling of joy and peace would be my constant companion through many trials and much pain, suffering, and persecution in the near future. I wanted my family to have that feeling too. I have learned that this feeling of joy is constant and unchangeable, exactly like Heavenly Father, whom I had come to know and love while attending BYU.

Left to right: the ward mission leader, a friend from the ward (Dave), me, Bryce.

I still remember the testimonies shared during my baptism. The witness offered by our dorm mom, Sister Boekweg, specifically touched me. She testified, "It has been given to me to know that Sahar has a great work to do here on the earth and that the testimony she has will grow within her, and she will do great work among her people."

After my baptism, my bishop laid his hands on my head to confirm me a member of the Church and grant me the gift of the Holy Ghost. I read about this gift in the Bible: "Now when the apostles which were at Jerusalem heard that Samaria had received the word of God, they sent unto them Peter and John: who, when they were come down, prayed for them, that they might receive the Holy Ghost: . . . Then laid they their hands on them, and they received the Holy Ghost" (Acts 8:14–15, 17). In the first century, the Apostles of Jesus Christ received this same gift from the Savior, who then authorized the Apostles through priesthood ordination to give this gift in the same way—by the laying on of hands— to others who were baptized. Although my bishop pronounced many wonderful blessings on me as he laid his hands on my head, the most important words to me were these: "Through the authority given to me, I confirm you a member of The Church of Jesus Christ of Latter-day Saints and say unto you, receive the Holy Ghost." The gift of the Holy

Ghost grants me the blessing of constant companionship with a member of the Godhead. This gift has blessed me with the possibility of keeping those feelings of peace and joy with me every day and every hour since my baptism. My bishop also blessed me with many other things, including something similar to the idea that Sister Boekweg had mentioned earlier: I would do a great work among my people. I didn't know what that meant at the time.

Five months after my baptism, I completed my graduate degree at BYU. I wanted to stay in the United States because I feared things may be hard for me in Palestine, especially now that I was a member of the Church. After sincere prayer, however, I knew through the Holy Ghost that Heavenly Father wanted me to return to Palestine.

I discovered that the political situation back home was not much different than it had been before I left. The outside world assumed that Palestinians could now govern their own affairs and were free; the reality was nothing like that. Our passports were recognized by very few countries. We continued to be denied access to most places within our own country. We were banned from crossing from Palestinian areas to Israeli areas. The cities governed under the Palestinian Authority were isolated and scattered all over Palestine, so getting from one city to another meant we had to travel on Israeli roads and pass through Israeli checkpoints, which was always difficult and often impossible. There was a high percentage of unemployment because those that worked in Israeli areas were now not allowed to get to work and those that worked in other Palestinian cities found it very difficult to commute.

My country seemed no better off than it had been two years earlier. The people were still depressed, poor, and struggling. There were still demonstrations, conflict, and agony. But one thing was different: my new life and my new perspective. So even though everything seemed the same, to me everything was different. I was able to find joy despite being surrounded by tragedy and was able to find strength and hope. It was a challenging time, yet the Holy Ghost was my constant companion, and those good feelings that I had experienced while at BYU remained with me.

When I returned to Palestine from BYU, I knew that I would face difficulty in obeying even the simplest commandments. Going to church was a challenge due to the travel restrictions imposed on Palestinians. The only LDS branch was at the BYU Jerusalem Center. Palestinians living in the West Bank are not allowed into Jerusalem, so getting to church each week was a challenge. I often had to sneak into Jerusalem, climbing hills and walls and hiding from Israeli soldiers. In addition to that, when I arrived back home as a converted member of The Church of Jesus Christ of Latter-day Saints, my family tried various means to convince me to leave the Church. This would continue hour after hour, day after day. They said that the Mormons had brainwashed me, that I was betraying my family and my faith, and that I was ruining their reputation in town.

A few short months after my baptism, I began to doubt that precious faith and the truths I had come to know and love. Despite many spiritual experiences confirming that I had done the right thing, I started to falter. After months of being the only member of the Church in my family and having everyone telling me I was wrong, I finally got to the point at which I didn't know anymore. I remember one hard night in particular, a few days before Christmas in 1996. My brother had spent all day mocking my beliefs and saying bad things about the LDS Church. He did this all day and continued even as I got in bed to sleep. Even though I was trying to sleep, he still would not leave my side. Unable to take it any longer, I got out of bed and, in order to avoid my brother's words, went into the bathroom. I found myself kneeling down in the bathroom and, through my tears, asking, "Heavenly Father, are you really there?" I had reached a point where even His mere existence was not clear to me anymore.

I had an amazing, sacred spiritual experience that night that not only confirmed to me the existence of God but also reconfirmed to me that the teachings of the LDS Church were true. I never doubted again! After that night, nothing my family said or did could shake my faith. I knew that Heavenly Father was real and that He loved me and cared about me. I also knew that whenever I needed Him, He would be there to comfort and strengthen me. I knew He was my Father and I was His precious daughter.

The Savior tells us, "Come unto me, all ye that labour and are heavy laden, and I will give you rest. Take my yoke upon you, and learn of me; for I am meek and lowly in heart: and ye shall find rest unto your souls. For my yoke is easy, and my burden is light" (Matthew 11:28–30). I have come to experience Christ's invitation firsthand. I now know what it is like to follow Him and take His yoke upon me. I testify that His yoke is truly easy and His burden is truly light. When I started to follow Him, I felt that He shared my yoke, and so it was easier to carry. But He did not stop at that. I felt that my Savior went the extra mile and carried me during the most difficult times of my life when I didn't even have the strength to put one foot in front of the other. I testify that life is much easier when we follow Him, not because difficulties and trials suddenly disappear, but because when we follow Him, He strengthens us, comforts us, carries our yoke, and even lifts us on the way to His mansions above.

Chapter 6

GATHERED

"And even so will I gather mine elect from the four
quarters of the earth, even as many as will believe in
me, and hearken unto my voice" (D&C 33:6).

"كما أني سأجمع من اخترتهم من أركان الأرض الأربعة، حتى كل من
يؤمنون بي وينصتون لصوتي." (المبادئ والعهود ٣٣: ٦)

I arrived early for church at the ward I was attending in the United States. I was sitting on a bench alone when a woman in the ward came and sat next to me. She turned to me and asked, "You are from Israel, right?" Not wanting her to mistake me for an Israeli (as many do and start to speak to me with the few Hebrew words they know), I said one sentence clarifying that I was from Palestine and that I was not Israeli. She then said to me, "I think the president may have said some things to indicate that Americans don't support Israel, but I want you to know that I support Israel with all my heart." After a small discussion as to what she meant by saying that she "supports Israel," I realized that she blindly supported everything the Israeli government did. After talking to her for some time, she noticed that I was not taking her side in "supporting Israel." She seemed to get slightly upset because of that and told me that I can't be a good member of the Church unless I support Israel.

I have often been surprised by the unconditional support some

Americans give to Israel. The tear gas bombs and weapons that Israel uses on my people are often made in the US or paid for by the American government. I have seen those weapons kill children in Gaza and destroy houses, burying entire families underneath the rubble. Thousands of Palestinian civilians have been injured or killed in Gaza, and the hundreds of Palestinian children who have died there have seemed to have little or no value to the outside world. It has seemed almost as if the value of Palestinian lives is less than the value of the lives of Israelis, Americans, or others. Gaza has about two million Palestinians and has been under siege for years now. Ninety percent of the water in Gaza is not clean, people there have no electricity for about eight hours every day, people are poor, citizens are not allowed to leave Gaza, and few supplies are allowed in. Sadly, the American media often does not present that side of the story. More often than not, Palestinians are portrayed as the enemy.

The separation wall that has torn our lives apart and destroyed our economy was almost fully funded by the United States. Israel reports that the separation wall has increased security and reduced terrorist attacks against Jews. We, the Palestinians, have found that it has created nothing but greater loss of freedom. The wall has decimated an already struggling economy by further cutting off access to market outlets. Likewise, access to medical, educational, religious, and cultural services has been seriously curtailed or eliminated. The wall has also separated us from our main water sources, springs, seas, and rivers. Israel controls all water sources and allocates only a small amount for the Palestinian areas. Most Palestinians have access to running water only about two to four days a month, requiring us to store water for more than two weeks sometimes. If we use up our water, we can purchase it, but usually at prices most Palestinians can't afford.

Some may think that our opposition to the unjust actions of the Israeli government means that we are anti-Semitic. On the contrary, we, the Palestinians, have lived alongside Jews for years—they have been our close neighbors, and we know that there are countless good Jewish people throughout the world. My grandfather's best friend was Jewish.

Water storage tanks on top of Palestinian homes in the Bethlehem area.

Daphna and me at the bank of the Jordan River.

My cousin Rana says she remembers when that friend came to visit my grandfather's home one day. She felt the deep love the two friends had for each other as they embraced. Love and friendship can surely exist between Palestinians and Israelis. One of my really good friends, Daphna, is an Israeli member of the Church. She is an amazing person who loves the Lord and serves Him every day of her life. I sat with Daphna in the celestial room of the Provo Temple one day and thought, *This is what it is all about.* Here lies the solution to the Palestinian/Israeli conflict: People from both sides coming unto Christ and accepting Him as their Savior. Learning to let go of all the anger and hate, and embrace each other. Palestinians and Israelis alike being gathered into one fold and both looking unto the Savior as their King and Redeemer.

What the Israeli government is doing in Palestine is a simple apartheid system discriminating against the Palestinian Arabs. This comes from the strong influence Zionists have in the Israeli government. Zionists strive to establish a Jewish State in Palestine, and they believe non-Jews have no place in their Jewish State. This is why there have been many unjust acts of discrimination against the Palestinians (non-Jews) all over the country. Zionists do not represent the good Jews all over the world. Other Jewish people often do not agree with Zionist views. Even many Israeli Jews oppose the actions that the Israeli government is taking against the Palestinian people. During the multiple Israeli attacks on Gaza, some Jews demonstrated and demanded that the Israeli army stop the killing of innocent Palestinians.

It is important to see the situation in the Holy Land from a different side, a side that the media often does not show. Some things that you have been led to believe may not be true. As Mark Twain said, "If you don't [listen to the news] you are uninformed; if you [listen to the news] you are misinformed." For example, the photographs below may be something you would never see in the media. Pictures of Israelis siding with Palestinians or even demonstrating against the actions of the State of Israel are not often displayed.

President Hunter said, "Both the Jews and the Arabs are children of our Father. They are both children of promise, and as a Church we do not take sides. We have love for and an interest in each. The purpose of the Gospel of Jesus Christ is to bring about love, unity, and brotherhood of the highest order" ("All Are Alike Unto God," Brigham Young University Fireside, February 4, 1979).

I think part of the confusion some people have comes from the current name of the State of Israel. The word *Israel* in the Bible and the *State of Israel* are two different things, yet some mistake them as the same. The

My brother Mazin with a couple of Jewish friends.

Jews demonstrating against the State of Israel in support of the Palestinians.

name *Israel* in the Bible is a holy name. It means "triumphant with God" and is actually a good word, even though some try to pollute it. It is the name that was given by the Lord to Jacob: "And God said unto him, Thy name is Jacob: thy name shall not be called any more Jacob, but Israel shall be thy name: and he called his name Israel" (Genesis 35:10). Jacob was Abraham's grandson, and Jacob had twelve sons. In the Old Testament, we learn that the descendants of the twelve sons of Jacob (or Israel) became known as the twelve tribes of Israel, or the children of Israel. In the Old Testament, the Lord made a covenant with Abraham and his seed, and therefore with the twelve tribes of Israel. This covenant was conditional upon them keeping His commandments.

As part of that covenant, the land of Palestine was given to the "covenant people of God." At the time, the covenant people of God were the Israelites. God made a covenant with Abraham and told him that *if* his seed was faithful in keeping His commandments, they would inherit the land of Canaan. However, a covenant is a two-way promise. When we keep our end of the promise, the Lord keeps His. When we don't, we have no promise (see D&C 82:10). Heavenly Father made that clear to the children of Israel and warned them, saying, "And if ye will not for all this hearken unto me, but walk contrary unto me; then I will walk contrary unto you also in fury; and I, even I, will chastise you seven times for your sins. . . . And I will scatter you among the heathen, and will draw out a sword after you: and your land shall be desolate, and your cities waste" (Leviticus 26:27–28, 33). Despite all warnings, the children of Israel broke their covenant with God. They stopped being obedient and became rebellious. Because of that, they were scattered and driven out of their land of inheritance. However, the Lord promised that they will be gathered again one day, conditional upon them returning to Him, being obedient to His commandments, and believing in His Son, Jesus Christ:

"Wherefore, the Jews shall be scattered among all nations. . . . And after they have been scattered, and the Lord God hath scourged them by other nations for the space of many generations, yea, even down from generation to generation until they shall be persuaded to believe in Christ, the Son of God, and the atonement, which is infinite for all mankind—and when that day shall come that they shall believe in Christ, and worship the Father in his name, with pure hearts and clean hands, and look not forward any more for another Messiah, then, at that time, the day will come that it must needs be expedient that they should believe these things" (2 Nephi 25:15–16).

Some believe that the gathering of the Jews to the land of Palestine is the prophesied gathering of the children of Israel, but Elder Bruce R. McConkie clarified: "As all the world knows, many Jews are now gathering to Palestine, where they have their own nation and way of worship, all without reference to a belief in Christ or an acceptance of the laws and ordinances of his everlasting gospel. Is this the latter-day gathering of the Jews of which the scriptures speak? No! It is not; let there be no misunderstanding in any discerning mind on this point. This gathering of the Jews to their homeland, and their organization into a nation and a kingdom, is not the gathering promised by the prophets. It does not fulfill the ancient promises. Those who have thus assembled have not gathered into the true Church and fold of their ancient Messiah" (*The Millennial Messiah* [1982], 229).

So, what is this gathering that the scriptures speak of? The gathering mentioned in the scriptures is more of a spiritual gathering than it is a physical gathering. Although a physical gathering of the covenant people of the Lord will happen, there must be a spiritual gathering first. The restoration of the Church of Jesus Christ and the restoration of the keys of the priesthood commenced the gathering of Israel from the four corners of the earth. The children of Israel are the covenant people of the Lord, and many people have already been gathered into the fold as they have entered the waters of baptism and developed faith in Christ.

As unbelievers come unto Christ and make covenants with God, they are gathered into the house of Israel. In the Book of Mormon, we read, "For behold, I say unto you that as many of the Gentiles as will repent are the covenant people of the Lord; and as many of the Jews as will not repent shall be cast off; for the Lord covenanteth with none save it be with them that repent and believe in his Son, who is the Holy One of Israel" (2 Nephi 30:2).

From the LDS Bible Dictionary we learn that the word *Israel* could also mean "a true believer in Christ." Nearly 80,000 missionaries of the Church are going to every country proclaiming the gospel to all nations. People from all nationalities and locations are coming into the fold, "and there shall be one fold, and one shepherd" (John 10:16). The gathering of Israel mentioned in the Bible is not about the Jews going to Palestine. Instead, it refers to people from all over the world being gathered to the fold of the Good Shepherd.

God gathers His people to help them come closer to Him, have faith in Him, and make covenants with Him. That is partly why the early Saints were asked to gather in America in the early days of the Church. There they could build a temple, receive ordinances, and make covenants with God. When we follow the Savior and are baptized into His Church, we become part of the house of Israel. We become the people of God.

I feel very blessed to be of the house of Israel. When I received my patriarchal blessing, I was told that I am of the house of Israel. I was also told to be true to my lineage and my tribe. In addition to receiving that knowledge, the minute I walked into the Lord's house and made a covenant with Him, I knew that I became one of His covenant people. A few years ago, I had the privilege to translate the patriarchal blessings of many Arab members of the Church. I remember one blessing in particular in which a Palestinian sister was told that the blood of Benjamin runs in her veins and that she is a literal descendent of Jacob. I hope we all realize that we can be recipients of those same blessings given to Abraham. We are His seed and are children of the covenant.

President Joseph Fielding Smith said: "Every person who embraces the gospel becomes of the house of Israel. In other words, they become members of the chosen lineage, or Abraham's children through Isaac and Jacob unto whom the promises were made. The great majority of those who become members of the Church are literal descendants of Abraham through Ephraim, son of Joseph. Those who are not literal descendants of Abraham and Israel must become such, and when they are baptized and confirmed they are grafted into the tree and are entitled to all the rights and privileges as heirs" (*Doctrines of Salvation,* 3 vols., Salt Lake City: Bookcraft, 1954–56, 3:246).

We are all brothers and sisters. "[Heavenly Father] hath made of one blood all nations of men for to dwell on all the face of the earth, . . . that they should seek the Lord, if haply they might feel after him, and find him, though he be not far from every one of us: For in him we live, and move, and have our being; . . . For we are also his offspring" (Acts 17:26–28). As we come unto Christ and abide in His love, we can develop some of His attributes—attributes such as forgiveness, tolerance, love, patience, sacrifice. Then will He gather us, as a chicken gathers her chicks under her wings (see 3 Nephi 10:5).

I look forward to the day when the Jews and all of God's children will be gathered into the fold of God; when they will be converted and believe in their Savior, the Holy One of Israel; when they will know and understand that the Messiah has come. Then they will be gathered and the Lord will pour out blessings upon them.

The Savior loves each and every one of us. He is the true Messiah, the one whom the Jews rejected, and the same one whom the Jews await. He *did* come. He came to His own, and His own received Him not. He was rejected, persecuted, and crucified. Yet He lives today, and He will come again in His glory. He will part the clouds and appear from the East. All will see Him, all will recognize Him, and every tongue will confess that He is the Christ. Every knee will bow before Him, the King of Kings and Lord of Lords, the Savior of the world.

The Savior's love for all mankind is everlasting and perfect. He loves sinners and saints alike. All lives matter equally to Him. He has the same amount of love for the Arabs as He has for the Jews and the Americans and everyone else. He can teach us to love others as He does. There was a time in my life when my heart was full of anger and hate. The Savior softened my heart and helped me love and forgive even those that caused me pain. The Savior can heal our hearts and teach us how to see others through His eyes and have charity toward all mankind.

A Day in My Life 3

Background: A Palestinian was killed the day before, and curfew was imposed on my town. We were confined to our homes and not allowed to leave. This is a description of my trip to church.

In the early hours of that morning, deathly silence covered the town. No one dared walk out in the streets or even step outside their home. We were under curfew. Just hours before, the Israeli soldiers drove around the streets of our town announcing, "People of Beit Sahour, you are now under curfew until further notice. Those who leave their house will be severely punished." I have known people that have been shot simply because they went outside during days of curfew. I was assigned to give a talk in sacrament meeting that day. I got up and got dressed for church, but as to how I would get there, I had no idea.

During a curfew, no public transportation is available and walking along the streets is extremely dangerous. I decided that I could only step outside. That was all that I could do. I had faith that Heavenly Father, somehow, would do the rest. I knew not how He would do it. Amazingly enough, my mother, who often objected to me going to church, did nothing to prevent me from going that day. I think she knew that I wouldn't go far, as I couldn't walk all the way to Jerusalem. I opened the door and walked outside with my heart pounding so fast. In fear, and while exploring my surroundings, I stepped down the few steps that led from my front porch to the street.

The silence was good because it meant no soldiers were in sight. As soon as I reached the street, I heard the sound of a car, and to my relief it was not the sound of an army jeep but a Palestinian taxi. Where did it come from and where was it going? The taxi driver said he was going to Jerusalem, and he had others with him that needed to get there for medical reasons or for work. My family's house in Beit Sahour is on a small street where few cars pass by, and certainly no taxis. So when I spotted a taxi right at my doorstep and during curfew, I knew it was not a coincidence.

I got into the taxi and the driver drove off, avoiding the main roads, which were more likely guarded by soldiers. Once outside of Beit Sahour there were no side roads; from that point, only one main road leads to Jerusalem. So the taxi driver simply left the road and began driving through a hay field. Needless to say, it was a very rough and dusty ride. After driving across the field for some distance I started to feel regret for eating breakfast that morning. The heat and the dust and the shaking were too much. I sighed in relief when we found a rocky unpaved road. I was thrilled because even though it was unpaved, it was still a road. Our taxi had barely started down that dirt road when it was abruptly stopped. Blocking the road in front of us was a pile of dirt. The military had anticipated that we may try to travel on even these primitive roads, so they placed that pile of dirt and rocks to block it. My fellow passengers and I became discouraged and started to complain. But, not the taxi driver! He was equal to the challenge. With a determination borne of knowing that what he was doing was good—transporting needy people to their destinations—he scanned his surroundings and spotted the olive tree field adjacent to the pile of dirt. With only a little hesitation, he turned the taxi to face the field. We were amazed to see the finesse with which the taxi driver maneuvered around those olive trees and made it to the other side of the pile of dirt and back on our rocky, unpaved road again.

By the time we finally reached the next town, we were hot, sweaty, and frazzled, but really happy and grateful as we exited the cab. Typically, Palestinian taxis can drive only to Abu Dis (near Bethany), a Palestinian town just outside of Jerusalem, since no Palestinian cars are allowed inside Jerusalem proper. For this reason, getting from Abu Dis to Jerusalem is more challenging than getting from home to Abu Dis. In 2002, the separation wall was built across the city of Abu Dis, dividing the city into two. Getting around the wall and finding an open area to sneak in or climb the wall became increasingly difficult as the wall reached farther. That time, however, the twenty-five-foot concrete wall was not yet built, but there was a shorter ten-foot wall and a "gate." The gate had soldiers stationed near it checking the identity cards of those that walked into the gate. I took a taxi to the gate, then with confidence walked through. My heart almost stopped as I saw three soldiers asking people to stop and show them their papers. I said a silent prayer and walked forward, avoiding eye contact with the soldiers. As I got closer to the soldiers my heart pounded faster and faster until I passed by the soldiers. I looked back waiting for the soldiers to ask me to stop; they didn't. I watched as people walked through the gate. They were *all* stopped by the soldiers, but not me. I felt Heavenly Father had somehow made me invisible that day.

As I walked down the hill I saw a woman carrying a large, 70-lb. bag of flour. She said she had sneaked into the city a different way without the soldiers seeing her, but she was so tired and could not carry her flour bag. I stopped and helped her carry it. It was so heavy that I felt my muscles ache so badly towards the end of the road. I was happy to see a bus that could take us to Damascus Gate. On the way to Damascus Gate, the bus was stopped at a checkpoint. I thought that getting caught after all these miracles was not an option. The soldier got on the bus and checked everyone's identity card. He made everyone who didn't have a Jerusalem identity card get off the bus. Well, except me! He walked towards me, took my identity card in his hand, and looked at it. He then asked me, "Where are you from?" I said, "Beit Sahour." He looked at me, then looked at the identity card, folded it, and gave it back to me. I waited for him to say, "Get off the bus!" But he didn't. I watched all those Palestinians that were forced off the bus being lined up on the wall. The women were on one side and the men on the other. The soldiers started beating up the men. I closed my eyes to avoid seeing this scene and felt partially guilty that I was the lucky one who stayed on the bus. I wanted so bad to get off the bus and try to stop that soldier, but I knew that would not do any good. The bus started its engine and drove away. My eyes were fixed back at those people left behind. My heart ached for them.

I got to Damascus gate, then took a bus to the Mount of Olives, then walked up the hill to the Jerusalem Center. As I walked in, a member of the branch saw me and approached me. "I am glad you are here. I am glad they let you through," she said. *Let me through?* That does not even begin to explain what happened. "Thank you," I said, not wanting to give her the lengthy version.

Another member of the branch approached me and said, "Hi, are you visiting?" Because it was often weeks before I could attend church, I was often mistaken for a visitor by short-term members of the branch. As a result, I sometimes felt disconnected from members. I shared a few of my experiences with some, but mostly what I shared was brief. That day during my talk I did mention briefly that I had to drive in a hay field and that the taxi driver managed to get us through.

Chapter 7

CHARITY

*"Ye have heard that it hath been said, Thou shalt love
thy neighbour, and hate thine enemy. But I say unto
you, Love your enemies" (Matthew 5:43–44).*

"سَمِعْتُمْ أَنَّهُ قِيلَ: تُحِبُّ قَرِيبَكَ وَتُبْغِضُ عَدُوَّكَ. وَأَمَّا أَنَا فَأَقُولُ لَكُمْ: أَحِبُّوا
أَعْدَاءَكُمْ" (متى ٥: ٤٣–٤٤)

It was a beautiful day in the spring of 1997, almost a year after I had
joined the Church. I woke up early and looked out my window at the
beautiful sunrise. The fluffy clouds were glowing with vibrant orange and
red, and I could hear the birds playing on the olive tree beside my window. I picked up my scriptures from my bedside and read a few chapters
from the Bible and the Book of Mormon. At about 6:00 a.m. my mother
walked into my room and saw me reading my scriptures. "Stop reading
this nonsense," she said. "I am going to burn those scriptures so that you
can't read them anymore." What she said seemed to pierce my heart,
even though this was one of the many times she had said the very same
thing to me. I got up and proceeded to get ready for church. I had some
breakfast, picked up my purse, and began to leave.

As I walked toward the front door of our house, my mother said,

"I just heard on the news that the roads are closed today. They won't allow you into Jerusalem. You should not try."

I smiled and said, "Well then, Mom, I will be back soon."

I walked the two blocks toward the city center so I could catch a taxi to the Bethlehem checkpoint. I had to wait for ten minutes or so, but a yellow taxi finally came. This was one of the shared taxis that people take together to save money. All seven of us in that taxi were heading to Jerusalem. We got out of the taxi at the Israeli checkpoint (Palestinian taxis are not allowed into Jerusalem). At that time, the checkpoint was primarily a roadblock. The soldiers made a long pathway for Palestinians to form a line and present their papers to authorize entry. The pathway was fenced, and I felt like I was inside a cage as I walked through it. Many tired people complained about the long wait. I could hear arguing going on at the front of the line from people who were being turned back for not having the proper papers. Feelings of frustration and anger rushed through my mind. The sound of the birds, the beautiful sunrise, and the spirit I had felt as I had read my scriptures that morning seemed to vanish as the sounds of angry voices escalated.

I was one of the many without the right papers to enter Jerusalem. Some people in line with me had work permits or medical reports showing they needed to get to a hospital, but I had nothing—nothing except faith that Heavenly Father would soften the hearts of the soldiers to let me pass. It was finally my turn, and I approached the soldier with confidence, only to hear him yell, *"Rokh 'Al-Beit"* ("Go home!") and tell me that I was not allowed into Jerusalem.

I looked up at this nineteen-year-old soldier, who had a fair complexion and blue eyes. He was obviously someone who had recently immigrated to my country. Here he was, a stranger in my country, telling me that I was not allowed to enter Jerusalem, the city of my birth. His army-green attire and his M-16 rifle obviously gave him the power to decide who got into and who stayed out of Jerusalem. If I turned around now, I would have to go around the back way (taking another two hours—that is, assuming I even made it). I looked at my watch, and it showed that the time was approaching 8:30. That meant that if I went the back way, I would miss partaking of the sacrament, since our services started at 10:00 a.m.

"I need to go to church. Please let me in," I said.

Acting like he didn't hear me, the soldier yelled even louder, "*Rokh 'Al-Beit.*"

Frustration rushed through my whole body as I looked into his uncaring blue eyes. It did not matter to him why I needed to go through the checkpoint or whether or not I had good intentions.

Israeli soldier turning people back at one of the Israeli checkpoints in Palestine.

Courtesy Justin McIntosh.

As I thought about what to say in order to convince him, feelings of hate, anger, and impatience overpowered me. It was then that I remembered a scripture I had read that morning. The words came clearly and penetrated deep down into my heart; they were the words of the Savior: "Ye have heard that it hath been said, Thou shalt love thy neighbour, and hate thine enemy. But I say unto you, Love your enemies, bless them that curse you, do good to them that hate you, and pray for them which despitefully use you, and persecute you; That ye may be the children of your Father which is in heaven" (Matthew 5:43–45). I wondered why these particular words came to my mind at that moment. Suddenly I had the impression that these words were a commandment from my Savior telling me to love my enemies.

I paused and stood there, almost breathless, as those words rang in my ears over and over. I looked at the soldier, who was still standing there waiting for me to leave. *Love my enemies?!* What? How could that be possible? I knew that the Lord's words had come to my mind for a reason. My initial thought was, *The Lord couldn't possibly expect me to love these soldiers!* After the terrible acts of injustice that I had seen some of the soldiers do, He could not possibly expect me to love *them!*

As a child I'd had a fear of the Israeli soldiers. My young mind looked at their guns and military outfits and shivered in fear when I saw them. I went to a girls' school two blocks away from my house in Beit Sahour. It had primary and secondary grades. Sometimes there were demonstrations at the school, organized by the older girls. On the playground, the girls held up signs with slogans on them and protested the Israeli occupation. The principal made us, the younger girls, stay in the classrooms. The Israeli soldiers would come and fire tear gas at the girls on the playground.

Once, when I was in the fifth grade, we heard gunshots and smelled tear gas but simply waited inside until everything was calm. I can still picture the fear on my friends' faces when a student opened our classroom door and a tear gas bomb rolled inside. A teacher quickly threw it out of the classroom and shut the door. But with the horrible effects of the tear gas and the shock of seeing the bomb in front of us, we all panicked. Our teachers did their best to calm us down, without success. I remember one of my classmates, Fadia, curled up in the corner of the classroom screaming uncontrollably, constantly asking for her mommy. We all wanted to go home and be in the safe arms of our mothers—but that was not permitted until the shooting stopped. Long hours of waiting in fear at my school are still vivid in my memory.

After long hours of waiting, our teacher finally announced that we were free to go home. This was good news, but there was still the difficult task of leaving the safety of our classroom to go outside where the soldiers were. I knew that we had to pass the soldiers in the street to get to our homes. My young mind thought that those soldiers, who hours earlier had shot at the other schoolgirls, could very well shoot me, too. As I passed by them, my heart beat so fast and so loud that I thought the soldiers could hear it and sense my fear.

Now, years later, here I was standing before a similar soldier at the checkpoint, and several more memories flooded my mind. One image from my teenage years would not leave me. It was the image of the lifeless body of my fellow student, Isaac, shot in the head by the Israeli soldiers. It was that particular incident that made my hate for these soldiers so strong. A spark that kindled when I was a teenager had grown to a massive fire of hate that engulfed me and numbed my every attempt to extinguish it. It might be possible to overcome the humiliation, loss of identity, and injustices, but there was no way I could ever forgive nor forget the act of cruelty committed against Isaac. This was another trial of my commitment to Jesus Christ. I was being asked to love those very soldiers who unjustly killed Isaac and desecrated his body.

Suddenly awakened from these ten-year-old memories of Isaac's death, I found myself still facing one of those soldiers who had taken away my land and who was now denying me entry into the city of my birth. How could Heavenly Father expect me to forgive him and even *love* him? Surely the Lord could see that this was simply not possible considering all the pain the soldiers had caused me and my people. Shocked by what I had just been commanded to do, I had no power to argue with the solider, and with a heavy heart I turned around to go home. I walked through the fenced pathway that led out of the checkpoint. I looked back at the soldiers and saw that they were turning many people back and denying them entry to Jerusalem. Women were arguing with the soldiers—some telling them that they had to go to the hospital, and some saying they must go to work—but with a rude voice the soldier told them what he had told me a few moments earlier: *"Rohk 'al Beit."* Despite the commotion behind me, as I walked away from the checkpoint, all I could hear were the words "love your enemies" still repeating in my ears. At that moment, it became clear to me that this was a commandment from my Savior, just like any other commandment. He was asking me to love and forgive the Israeli soldiers who brought me and my people so much pain.

Why would the Savior give me a commandment that He knew I could not obey? I thought. I believed that when He gave me a commandment,

He would also provide a way to obey it like He did for Nephi (see 1 Nephi 3:7). Even though I knew that principle to be true, every attempt on my part to love and forgive these soldiers was in vain. My hard heart simply could not do it! I prayed for guidance and help but could not feel any change in my feelings. I thought about how I was currently preparing to go through the temple for the first time. *How could I enter the Lord's house without being obedient to* all *the commandments?*

After days of spiritual turmoil and confusion, I was led to read Moroni 7:48: "Wherefore, my beloved brethren, pray unto the Father with all the energy of heart, that ye may be filled with this love, which he hath bestowed upon all who are true followers of his Son, Jesus Christ; that ye may become the sons of God; that when he shall appear we shall be like him, for we shall see him as he is; that we may have this hope; that we may be purified even as he is pure." I felt the prophet Mormon's words were directed to me. Those words sank deep into my heart, and I pondered them day after day. I realized that charity was a gift from God. All I had to do was desire to have it with all my heart, and then I could pray to my Heavenly Father, and He would give me this divine gift.

Could the Savior really teach me how to love? I knew that I could not find love for those soldiers, nor could I forgive them, by my efforts alone. My mortal heart simply could not let go of the past. I needed the Atonement. I needed the Savior's enabling power and His perfect love to fill my heart. The Savior's last words as He hung on the cross in agony were, "Father, forgive them; for they know not what they do" (Luke 23:34). In this astonishing example, the Savior was able to forgive the soldiers that had crucified Him! He not only forgave them, but He also prayed for them! The soldiers I was trying to forgive certainly didn't whip me or crucify me, so how could I justify not forgiving them? Clearly, there was someone who knew how to forgive and love, and that was my Savior and Redeemer.

Mormon helped me realize that charity was a gift from God. I know now that Heavenly Father is the source of all love. The process of gaining charity is similar to that of gaining faith. We must plant and nourish that seed of faith so that it will grow (see Alma 32). But where does that seed of faith originate? We certainly don't create it. That seed is the word of God that a loving Father in Heaven freely gives us. Even when we only desire to have faith in His word, the Lord gives us the seed to nourish (see Alma 32:27). I realized that the same principle applied to charity. When our hearts are unable to forgive and love, there is help from above. If I want to have charity, I must do three things: First, I must desire to have charity. Second, I must pray with "all the energy of heart" in order to obtain charity (Moroni 7:48). Third, I must have faith that Heavenly Father can teach me how to love. I gained strength to succeed from the Savior's example.

I determined to ask Heavenly Father for help. I knelt down and prayed. I must say that I was disappointed, because I expected a miraculous change in my heart and my feelings right away. That did not happen. I continued to fast and pray, being confident that one day my prayer would be answered.

My heart was so hard that it took months for Heavenly Father to mold it and soften it. Almost a year after that event, I was heading to church on a normal Sabbath. I was prepared to be turned back, as the Bethlehem checkpoint had gotten even harder to cross. I still waited and hoped, just as I had almost a year earlier. The soldier at the checkpoint was not allowing anyone in that day. He demanded that everyone leave and said no one could enter. I looked at the fathers who were eager to go to Jerusalem to work in order to obtain food for their families, at the children who were in school attire with their backpacks on, and at the many others who were carrying medical records and x-rays. My heart broke for them because, for me, it was only church that I would be missing.

"Everyone, go home," I heard the soldier repeat. At this same place, just a year earlier, I had heard the Savior's inviting commandment to love my enemies. Now, as I looked up at the soldier's face, I expected to find the same hate and anger that I had found last year. This time, however, my heart seemed different. As I looked into the soldier's eyes, my heart filled with love instead of hate. These feelings of love shocked me. I had been unaware of the gradual change in my feelings, and I still questioned my ability to love these soldiers. But as I looked at that solider that day, I saw a brother of mine—a brother not only because Palestinians and Israelis are literally related by blood but also because in front of me stood a son of God, beloved of Him. I could feel Heavenly Father's love for that soldier. In my mind, I was able to isolate every bad thing I had seen the soldiers do. I still hated those acts, but my hate for the soldiers themselves was gone. I was finally able to love my enemies! Like Jesus forgave the Roman soldiers who nailed Him to a cross, I could love those soldiers who hurt my people. This feeling of charity and forgiveness did not come from me. These feelings were given to me because of my faith in the Atonement of Jesus Christ and because I trusted in Him and asked for His help. It was the Savior that filled my heart with His love.

Corrie Ten Boom, a Christian who hid Jews from the Nazis and survived their concentration camp, wrote of her encounter with one of the guards: "I discovered that it is not on our forgiveness any more than on our goodness that the world's healing hinges, but on His. When He tells us to love our enemies, He gives, along with the command, the love itself" (*The Hiding Place,* by Corrie ten Boom, John Sherrill, and Elizabeth Sherrill [Bantam edition, 1974], 238.

From this experience, I learned that I could love others, even those who had hurt me and my loved ones. The only way to do this is with the Savior's help. The Savior is my example: He is the only one who suffers long, envies not, and thinks no evil (see 1 Corinthians 13). Mormon tells us, "Wherefore, my beloved brethren, if ye have not charity, ye are nothing, for charity never faileth. Wherefore, cleave unto charity, which is the greatest of all, for all things must fail—But charity is the pure love of Christ, and it endureth forever; and whoso is found possessed of it at the last day, it shall be well with him" (Moroni 7:46–47).

As Mormon so clearly testifies, I also testify that charity is essential for our spiritual well-being. It is essential not only because it is a commandment from God to love others but also because letting go of anger and hate is liberating. One day, my friends and I waited in line for a very long time to cross the Qalandia checkpoint. We waited in multiple lines for an hour or so each, and each time, when it was our turn, the soldier at the gate would say, "This path is closed. Go to a different line." After this happened two or three times, one of my friends got very upset. Later she asked me, "How can you deal with this injustice and not get angry?" I told her that if I let myself get angry each time something like this happened, I would be angry all my life. As I have learned to love my enemies, I have also realized that at some point in your life, you have to learn to let go. Being angry and hateful toward others only hurts you. My faith and feelings of peace have intensified by learning to love and forgive as exemplified by our Savior Jesus Christ.

Elder Joseph B. Wirthlin said: "We should sow within our hearts the seed of charity, the pure love of Christ. He is the perfect model of charity. His total life, particularly his atoning sacrifice, is a lesson in charity. His every act reflects absolute, unequivocal love for all mankind and for each one of us. His example teaches us that charity means subordinating personal interests willingly and gladly for the good of others. I believe our progress toward exaltation and eternal life depends upon how well we learn and live the principle of charity. Charity must become a fundamental state of mind and heart that guides us in all we do" ("Seeds of Renewal," *Ensign,* May 1989).

In order to attain a higher degree of charity, I had to rely on my faith in the Savior, who is the perfect model of charity. Faith in Him helped me develop qualities that are closer to His. I had always believed that I had enough faith, but I came to realize that my understanding of faith was not complete and that I still had a lot to learn.

Chapter 8
FAITH

"If ye have faith as a grain of mustard seed, ye shall say unto this mountain, Remove hence to yonder place; and it shall remove; and nothing shall be impossible unto you" (Matthew 17:20).

"لَوْ كَانَ لَكُمْ إِيمَانٌ مِثْلُ حَبَّةِ خَرْدَلٍ لَكُنْتُمْ تَقُولُونَ لِهَذَا ٱلْجَبَلِ: ٱنْتَقِلْ مِنْ هُنَا إِلَى هُنَاكَ فَيَنْتَقِلُ، وَلَا يَكُونُ شَيْءٌ غَيْرَ مُمْكِنٍ لَدَيْكُمْ."

(متى ١٧: ٢٠)

My friend Jessica paid for my ticket to Utah so that I would be able to go through the temple for the first time. My ticket was for August 2, 1997. I was excited to go back to Utah, to see old friends, and to go to the house of the Lord. Although this is not possible anymore, in 1997, some Palestinians were allowed to fly out of the Tel Aviv airport, provided that they could obtain a permit from the Israeli authorities. The rest had to travel by land to Jordan and fly out of Amman. I was happy that I had obtained a permit from the authorities, and I was ready to leave from the Tel Aviv airport.

One day before I left, there was a bombing in Jerusalem. Israel announced that no Palestinian would be allowed to leave the country. I thought that having a ticket and a permit meant that I would be able to travel despite these new restrictions. Surely the authorities knew how hard obtaining that permit was. I asked some of my American friends from church to take me to the airport because even though I had a permit to travel, no one else in my family did, so they could not accompany me. Besides, Palestinians in the West Bank could not drive their cars on certain roads in Israeli areas.

I headed toward the Bethlehem checkpoint with my friends, trusting that, because I was going to the temple, the Lord would help me get there. The soldier at the checkpoint looked at my passport and permit and said that I was not allowed to leave Bethlehem. We argued with him, showing him my ticket and passport, and when he continued to refuse us entry, we asked to speak to his supervisor. Finally, I was allowed through the checkpoint, and we all smiled in relief. Then at the airport, the security guard at the gate would not allow me into the airport. The officer held out my passport and yelled, "No flights for this passport!" Again, it took a bit of effort, but we finally managed to convince him to allow me in. Now that I was at the airport, my friends felt they could leave.

I approached the officer inside the airport. She asked me many questions: "Did you pack your own bags? Did you buy something that you don't know the contents of? Do you have any bombs? Where are you going? Why?" When she was done asking questions, she gave me back my passport and said, "There are no flights for this passport." *What?* Why did she ask all these questions then? I didn't know what to do. My ride had left, and the time for my flight was getting closer and closer.

I thought I would try another security officer. It was the exact same story. He asked me the same questions, and after he finished asking questions, he announced, "You can't travel today!"

I was devastated. Why would I not be allowed to travel when I was going to the house of the Lord? Why would this happen to me? I called my friends and told them what had happened. Shortly after that phone call, I suddenly had a great feeling of peace come over me. I knew that I was not supposed to travel that day and that it would be all right. I later learned that after I had hung up the phone, my friends had all knelt down to pray for me. I felt the power of that prayer.

As much as I wanted to go to the temple that day, Heavenly Father

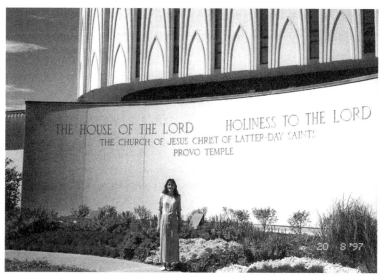

The day I received my endowment at the Provo Utah Temple.

knew I was not quite ready. We often think that strong faith means that we will be able to get what we need or want if we pray for it. Sometimes miracles happen: our prayers are answered, and we get what we need when we think we need it. On the other hand, sometimes God requires us to wait for the miracles and does not grant them right away, or even at all. For me, the wait made the experience of going to the temple all the sweeter.

When I finally entered the Provo Temple, two weeks after that hard experience at the airport, I felt that I had found the one place on earth that I belonged. Everyone was dressed in white, and I felt welcomed. In the temple it did not matter that the color of my skin was different or that I spoke a different language or that I was Palestinian. I was in the Lord's house, and I was His daughter. It was peaceful, quiet, and safe.

I have often considered myself to be a person of strong faith. I feel that my faith has allowed me to witness many miracles in my life. I have been protected, and I have been able to make it to church many times despite the checkpoints, curfews, and hardships. An old Muslim woman, however, once taught me a lesson about faith that helped me realize that my own faith was still small.

I met her one day while traveling to church. We were both stopped at a checkpoint, and everyone else in the taxi van had a permit to enter Jerusalem—everyone except for this elderly Muslim woman and me. The soldiers quickly identified the two of us and commanded us to get out of the taxi and return the way we had come. Trying to be helpful, the taxi driver advised us to cross the street and try to pass through at the other side of the checkpoint. Personally, I did not think it was a smart idea for many reasons. For one, the road was only about forty feet wide, so it was almost impossible not to be noticed. And there were eight soldiers stationed at the checkpoint, all of whom certainly saw us being kicked out of the taxi. So how would they allow us to cross?

The Muslim woman looked at me with her black eyes and said, "Let us try." I looked at her face. It was covered with wrinkles, and her gray hair showed slightly from underneath her white veil. Despite her age, I could tell she was a strong woman. Reluctantly, I followed this insistent old woman, mainly so I could prove that what we were about to do was pointless. While walking to the other side of the road, I heard this sweet woman repeat the words: "God, please distract the soldiers so we can pass." Although I was amazed at her faith, I could not imagine how this would work. We calmly walked to the other side of the road and began crossing through the checkpoint roadblocks only a few feet away from the soldiers who had just denied us entry. As I continued walking, I anticipated a yell from one of the soldiers at any moment, commanding us to turn back. We kept walking and walking . . . silence. No one noticed us. No one stopped us. Thanks to the faith of one remarkable Muslim woman who trusted that God could distract eight soldiers, I succeeded in my quest to worship Jesus Christ at my church with my fellow members that day.

This sweet woman taught me about true faith. She taught me that even when something seems impossible, you should still believe it can happen. The Savior tells us, "If ye have faith as a grain of mustard seed, ye shall say unto this mountain, Remove hence to yonder place; and it shall remove; and nothing shall be impossible unto you" (Matthew 17:20).

However, later in my life I discovered that faith does not mean that you always get what you want or even what you need. Sometimes faith means accepting the will of the Lord, because it is always better than our own will and desire. When my brother-in-law Hazim was diagnosed with cancer at the young age of fifty-three in 2010, I followed the example of the Muslim woman and prayed that he would be healed. I knew that it would require a miracle for Hazim to be healed, but I had been taught to believe in miracles. I felt that I had the necessary faith and that if I prayed hard enough, Hazim would be healed. I thought that my small faith, even though not strong enough to remove mountains, would be strong enough to heal a sick person. As I prayed and pleaded with the Lord with all my heart, the Lord told me that Hazim would die and that his death would strengthen my sister and her four children. Heavenly Father was saying no to my request for a miracle. He was telling me that this particular mountain was not meant to be removed.

Sometimes our mountains are not removed. It may be the wisdom of God that we climb those mountains and pass through those rocky, difficult roads. The faith needed to climb our mountains is actually greater than the faith needed to remove them. I often had to climb hills, mountains, and walls in order to get to church. My faith did not enable me to remove those obstacles or trials from my path. But Heavenly Father has given me the courage and strength to pass through them. Because I have done so, my faith has grown stronger.

As the Savior walked on the water and approached His disciples in the boat on the Sea of Galilee, He said to them, "Be of good cheer; it is I; be not afraid" (Matthew 14:27). The Lord bid Peter to come to Him, and Peter walked on the water toward the Savior: "But when he saw the wind boisterous, he was afraid; and beginning to sink, he cried, saying, Lord, save me. And immediately Jesus stretched forth his hand, and caught him, and said unto him, O thou of little faith, wherefore didst thou doubt?" (Matthew 14:30–31). Peter was an ordinary man, yet the Lord enabled him to do an extraordinary thing: to walk on water. Peter started to sink because of the storm that surrounded him. Many of us often lose our faith when we are faced with the storms of adversity. However, you will notice that when Peter feared, the Savior did not stop the winds, the waves, and the storm. Instead He reached out His hand and pulled Peter up. He does the same for us in our lives. He often does not calm the storms around us, but He gives us strength to go through them. He stretches forth His mighty arm and lifts us, bidding us not to doubt. Until I heard this experience related by my friend Camille, I had never noticed the next verse. Verse 32 says, "And when they were come into the ship, the wind ceased." When we allow the Savior into our lives, we feel peace and comfort and strength.

I know that difficult things are placed in our path for a reason. As we face mountains in our path, may we remember that these mountains are there to strengthen us and fortify our faith as we climb them with the Lord by our side. His work and His glory is to bring to pass our salvation. Nothing He does and nothing He allows to happen will harm us permanently. All our difficulties and hardships are there to strengthen us, refine us, and make us more like our Father in Heaven. When we face our daily mountains, may we not wish for them to be gone but pray for courage, strength, and faith to climb them.

Some of the hardest trials I have faced in my life were not checkpoints or political turmoil. They were the death of loved ones. Those were some mountains that I knew could not be removed. But with the Lord's hand in mine, enabled by the strength He gave me, I was able to climb even those rocky mountains.

Chapter 9
HOPE

*"He breaketh the bands of death, that the grave shall
have no victory, and that the sting of death should be
swallowed up in the hopes of glory" (Alma 22:14).*

"إِنَّهُ يَكْسِرُ أَغْلَالَ الْمَوْتِ فَلَا يَكُونُ لِلْمَوْتِ غَلَبَةٌ، وَتَتَوَارَى شَوْكَةُ
[الموت] فِي رَجَاءِ الْمَجْدِ" (ألما ٢٢: ١٤)

In 1998, I started working as a teacher at a university in Hebron. It was the only job I was able to find. Sadly, as at many other schools, classes were taught on Saturday, which was the day LDS Church services were held in Jerusalem. Most businesses and schools in Palestine have two days off every week. Since the two main religions among the Palestinians are Islam and Christianity, one of those is Friday, the Muslim Sabbath, and the other is Sunday, the Christian Sabbath. I still felt that I should take this job and often managed to schedule my classes in the afternoon on Saturday so I could attend sacrament meeting in the morning. It took me two hours to get from Jerusalem to Hebron, but only if I could get a ride halfway. I had a sweet couple in my branch, JoAn Berrett and her husband, who drove me from the Jerusalem Center to the Bethlehem checkpoint every Saturday so I could make it to class.

In early 2000, I was offered a job working at a tourist agency. The job was stationed in Jerusalem, paid a higher salary, and also provided me with a permit so I could enter Jerusalem "legally." I was thrilled to be able to go to church freely. However, it was short-lived because by the end of that same year, the second uprising erupted, which was called Al Aqsa Uprising. This started due to a provocative visit by the Israeli Prime Minister at the time, Ariel Sharon, to the Aqsa Mosque. He was accompanied by a significant number of Israeli forces and security personnel. The Muslims rose up in revolt because they considered this visit a desecration of their holy site and a political statement claiming that site for the Jews.

The political situation worsened, and a closure was imposed forbidding even those with permits, like me, from entering Jerusalem. I tried to sneak in to go to work, but my place of employment was very close to the checkpoint, just on the Jerusalem side. So, if I went around the back way, I would spend three hours just to get to the other side of the checkpoint, a few yards from where I had started, making a big circle. It was exhausting, so I decided I needed to find another job. But finding work in Palestine during the uprising was almost impossible.

I considered another option—going back to school. Tuition at BYU was less expensive than at other universities, especially for members of the Church, so I chose to do another degree at BYU. Since the university did not offer a PhD in statistics, I decided that maybe doing another degree in a field with high demand, like computer science, would help me find work faster.

I arrived in Utah in August 2001 and started my master's degree in computer science at BYU. Being away from my family was hard, especially after I heard that my uncle Yacoub was hospitalized with a serious condition. It was only a few days after I had arrived that I heard about his illness.

As I hung up the phone one day after talking with my cousin Rana in Beit Sahour, I had a feeling that my uncle would die. My uncle Yacoub is my father's younger brother. He is an amazing man who devoted his life to the field of education and environmental awareness. He was also kind and caring and always helped and gave encouragement to members of his family. He was the Director of Schools for twenty years and had a passion for altering the traditional form of teaching, helping children learn in nontraditional ways, through exploring and experimenting. His innovative methodology and his love for the students changed lives. His sudden illness was shocking to every one of us. It was hard for me to be so far away from my family during this difficult time. I could not stop the tears from rolling down my cheeks when I knew that I would not see my uncle Yacoub again. I cried that day until I could not breathe. My uncle died on September 7, 2001. I didn't realize it then, but the following months would bring more sorrow to me and my family.

To help pay the bills, I worked two jobs at BYU while going to school. My computer science classes also took a lot of time and energy. I found myself often sleep-deprived, weary, and depressed. A few months after my uncle's death, my mother called to tell me that my father was not feeling well. She said that they were doing some tests to find out what was wrong. I hung up the phone and immediately knew that my father's illness was serious. The test results showed evidence of two critical conditions: leukemia and a sizable growth in his lungs. Because the leukemia was the doctors' greatest concern, the lung tumor was temporarily ignored.

My next decision was an easy one: I knew I needed to be home for my father's treatment. I left BYU at the end of the semester and went home to be with him and the rest of my family during this difficult time. Upon my return to Beit Sahour, I was met with a cloud of gloom that covered my entire family. Everyone was depressed and very sad. I quickly recognized that I would have to be strong and work to help them have hope. Interestingly, despite the gloomy atmosphere, my father remained positive and full of hope. He was committed to beating the disease, shouldering whatever discomfort and pain it involved, and returning to health. He was the strength of our family. He knew how to fix everything that went wrong—mechanical or emotional. The disease was simply one new challenge to be fixed. He would defeat this cancer.

My father started chemotherapy in the Hadassah Hospital in

Jerusalem. Hadassah was the best hospital in Palestine/Israel, and naturally, my father wanted the best treatment. He needed a permit from the Israeli government to cross checkpoints to enter Jerusalem to go to the hospital. As his family, we also needed our own permits to visit him while he was a patient there. Obtaining these permits required significant time and plenty of evidence of need, but we all managed to get them. The permits were not good indefinitely; they expired after a few days, making it necessary to frequently repeat the process.

Treatment at the hospital was expensive. Each day that my father stayed at the hospital cost $500, equaling his entire retirement salary. Fortunately, our pleas for help resulted in financial assistance from then-Palestinian President Yassir Arafat, paying for half our medical expenses. Due to the crippling cost of hospital care, we could not have managed without Arafat's help.

Those days at the hospital passed very slowly; they were especially hard for my father. My mother was always with my father at the hospital. At the time, my mother owned about 450 lovebirds. Yes, that's right—450 little parakeets. My mother loves animals, but she mostly loves to see animals breed. So having one pet never satisfies my mom. They have to be in pairs, and they must reproduce. Her love for that specific type of lovebird grew when she discovered that they would have baby birds with magnificent colors. She would pair them up and wait patiently until the chicks hatched so she could see the beautiful combination of colors that resulted. She would start with a pair or two, but in a matter of a few months, she would have many of them. We kept them in the basement in cages, two per cage (unless they had babies). Over the years, she has discovered the best kinds of food and the best ways to keep her birds healthy and happy. Her secret mix of rice, eggs, cookies, and vegetables was magical. We even had friends bring their birds to stay with my mother for a few days so they could hatch and become healthier.

My siblings and I were not too fond of the birds. They were noisy and smelly and required constant care. We constantly encouraged my mother to sell them. But they were her babies, and she was not willing to

Back road leading from the south of the West Bank to the north,
which represents the only road that connects southern Palestinian cities
to northern cities on which Palestinians are allowed to travel.

sell any of them. That is why the birds would simply increase in number
as time went by. When my father was in the hospital, my mother was
not there to take care of her birds. So it became my job to feed the birds,
clean the cages, and give them fresh water every day. When I did this,
I took three times as long as my mother. This process took me almost
seven hours every day. At first, with pressure from my other siblings,
I contemplated selling some of the birds to make the work easier. But
after taking care of the birds for a few days, I grew attached to them and
refused to sell any. I soon discovered the reason my mother loved the
noisy little birds.

I began teaching at Bethlehem University in the fall of 2002. A few
months later, I received a better job offer from the Arab American
University in Jenin, a Palestinian city about fifty-five miles north of Beit
Sahour. Although it was hard for me to leave my father at this time,
we knew the chemotherapy treatment would last for months, and I

could still come home on weekends. Taking the interior road through Jerusalem, the fifty-five-mile drive from Bethlehem to Jenin should have taken an hour or so, but because of checkpoints and back roads, my weekend trip often took five hours each way. I often took taxis that detoured on dirt roads and through fields to avoid encounters with soldiers and checkpoints.

On one of my weekly trips after visiting my family, I could not find a taxi or a bus back to Jenin except from Ramallah. It took me about an hour and a half to get from Beit Sahour to Ramallah. After the Qalandia checkpoint (near Ramallah), I got in a taxi going to Jenin. Fifteen minutes after we left, the taxi was stopped at the Taybeh checkpoint. That day, there were five cars in front of us. The process took about half an hour per car. The soldiers at the checkpoint would ask everyone to get out of the car, check their identity cards, and then ask them to go back, letting no one across. Time passed slowly as we sat there in the sun, waiting for our turn so that we could be asked to go back—or so we thought! Finally it was our turn. We were shocked: they let us through when everyone else was turned back.

There was another checkpoint right after that one. We stopped and waited in line. At this checkpoint, the soldiers made everyone get out once again and checked their identity cards. And again they allowed us through the checkpoint. I got to Al-Zababdeh at 2:30 p.m. (after passing through seven checkpoints). The whole trip took seven hours, and I was so tired yet glad to be home. I noticed that our standards as Palestinians had shifted. We considered spending four hours on the road, crossing many checkpoints, getting searched and humiliated, a "fairly easy" trip. Even my seven-hour trip was not at all surprising to me. This was "normal" life as I knew it.

After months of treatment, the doctors announced that my father's leukemia was in remission. We celebrated with a big family party. But there was still that tumor in my father's lung, and the doctors were now ready to treat it. As soon as they began, however, they discovered that the tumor had grown and that they had likely waited too long. It was clearly another serious form of cancer. The first sign of trouble was my father's inability to move his right arm normally. Next, his speech became slurred. For my independent father, these changes were alarming, and he resisted accepting help from us for as long as possible. This was the hardest part of his illness for me—watching my father, who always gave help to others, require help for himself.

After more tests, doctors discovered another tumor—this one in his brain. They gave him two months to live. Slowly, my father lost his speech and his movement on the right side of his body. It was painful to watch this decline happen to the man who was the strength of our family. Only prayer and strength from the Lord kept me going during these difficult times. My brothers who lived in the States came home to be with our father during his final days. I longed for weekends, when I could come home to be with him as well.

Because of the high percentage of Muslim students at the Arab American University, the weekend consisted of Thursday and Friday (the Muslim Sabbath). After visiting Beit Sahour one weekend, I returned to Jenin and was about to start another week of classes. It was especially hard to leave my father that Saturday because he had a high fever and was not doing well. On Sunday morning, October 5, 2003, I woke up, and before I got ready for work, I prayed to Heavenly Father to end my father's suffering. I could not bear any longer the thought of him being in so much pain. I went to my classes that day, and later that morning, my brother-in-law Hazim called me and told me to come home. He didn't explain why, only that I should come home now. I taught my two classes for the day and tried to find a taxi to take me home. No direct public transportation between Jenin and Beit Sahour was available, so my best option was to hire a private taxi to take me to Beit Sahour. Sometime on that drive home, my nephew called and said, "*Salamit Rasik,*" which is a phrase that signifies that someone has died. No more needed to be said. I knew my father was gone.

After that phone call, many other family members called to see how far away I was and how long it would be before I could be home. It took about three hours for me to finally arrive. Nothing could have prepared me for the sight I encountered when I entered our house: about seventy women from our family, all dressed in black, were sitting in our living room, surrounding the casket that held my father's body. My sisters and mother were sobbing loudly, almost uncontrollably. I hugged each one briefly before my niece Lina led me to my room in the back of the house and handed me a few black shirts. "Choose one to wear," she directed me. I silently obeyed and reluctantly joined the grieving women in the living room.

I felt as though everyone was watching me to see my reaction. In contrast to the noise and confusion around me, my heart was at peace. I felt assured that my father was in a much better place and was finally free from the pain, restrictions, and discomfort of his disease-filled body. Many of the women thought I must be in shock because I showed no emotion. They felt I would do better if I cried and let out the anger and sadness. My aunt Rina even began to chant a sad song, trying to get me to cry. But I couldn't! Especially not with so many women watching me.

An hour later my brother Mazin left the group of men gathered on the second floor and asked to speak with me privately. Our garden in the back of the house was the "private" place at the time, because our house was full of people. He asked me, "Aren't you sad that Dad has passed away?"

I readily responded, "Of course I am!"

"Then why are you not crying?" he asked.

I told him that I believed our father was in a better place and that part of me was glad that he was finally at peace. My brother said, "You know I don't believe in God, but this morning, I had to wonder because right at the hour that dad died, the church bells rang. They don't normally ring at this time of day, but they did today." My brother was satisfied with my answer, and I felt I had had a spiritual moment as we escaped the gloomy room and went outside.

My father's funeral was that same afternoon. I was glad we didn't have to sit in that living room much longer. The men in our family came along with the priests from the Greek Orthodox church to offer prayers over my father's body and then to carry the coffin from the house to the church a few blocks away. All of us women followed. After the church service, which lasted an hour, the men carried the coffin to the graveyard to bury my father. My mother, my siblings, and I returned to the church hall, where we would remain for the next three days to greet people from our town who came to pay their respects.

The loss of my father was hard on me. In the mornings, I was accustomed to hearing him in the bathroom and then in the kitchen as he made his coffee. That first week after his death, I lay in bed still expecting to hear or see him. But he was gone. The tradition for women in Beit Sahour is to wear black for at least a year to show remembrance and sorrow after the death of a family member. The women of my family were no different. We all wore black and used no makeup on our faces. Cousins and aunts continued visiting our house every afternoon for forty days. Their company provided some consolation to my mother as I began worrying about leaving her when I returned to work in Jenin.

Life gradually seemed to go back to normal—or did it? In reality, everything had changed. The house seemed empty. The father I loved and respected was gone.

Because my cousin had lost her father two years before and still mourned his death, we talked about our fathers a lot. She would say, "I can't imagine that I won't ever see my father again."

And I would respond, "But you can!"

This is the beauty of the Atonement that our Savior made for us. We *will* see our loved ones again. One day I will see my father again; I will embrace him and live with him forever. I know with all my heart that because Christ was resurrected, we all will be as well. I know that my father will live once again and I will see him again. Without that hope, I, too, would have been devastated. This assurance of life after death gave me something to hold on to and helped me stay strong during these difficult times.

My family did not celebrate a traditional Christmas that year. For me, however, that Christmas was the most meaningful one of my life. Remembering why the Savior came to earth and what He did while here gave me strength. I knew that because the Savior walked out of His tomb that first Easter morning, my father, my uncle, my grandmother Milia and my grandfather Issa, and all my loved ones that had died would also walk out of their graves one day. That Christmas in 2003, I was so grateful for this knowledge. It kept me hopeful and helped me strengthen and support my family members. Thinking of my cousin's distress over her belief that she would never see her father again still brings me to my knees in gratitude for my belief in the reality of the Resurrection. I know with all my heart that my Savior lives. Because of Him, we all will live again.

I have experienced the deaths of many loved ones in my life, the latest of which were the deaths of both of my brothers-in-law in the same year. Days after my brother-in-law Hazim died in 2010, his four-year-old granddaughter Layar continued to go into his room. When asked why she was doing that, she said, "I go to see grandpa so I can sing to him."

My sister asked her, "What does grandpa say when you sing to him?"

"Nothing," Layar said. "He just smiles at me."

These events reaffirmed to me that life after death is real and that each of us has a divine mission in life. When we accomplish that mission, the time comes when we will leave this earth.

My sister often wonders, "Why? Why would someone as nice as Hazim die so young? He spent his life helping others. He was such a good person." Sometimes I think of mortal life as a university; if you are a good student, you graduate early. We come here to learn, grow, and pass tests, and then we graduate.

I had a teacher at BYU who gave really hard tests. He would announce, "This test is so hard that you will never be able to do it on your own." As we worked to complete the exam, he would interject hints to help us figure out the answers to the hard questions. When we asked why he created tests that were impossible without help, he explained, "Because I want you to learn from the test." I feel life is much the same; a main purpose of being here on earth is to learn from life's seemingly

My father's grave. My uncle Nasri's grave is on the right.

My family, January 1997. From left to right (seated on couch): Maher, Me, Samar, Father, Mother, Walid. Suhair is in the front kneeling, and Mazin is in the back behind my father.

impossible tests. We only truly succeed with help from our Savior and the Holy Ghost.

The Savior broke the bands of death. He rose triumphant from the dark grave. Because of His Atonement, whatever darkness we face on this earth is only temporary. All tests we face, whether they be death, sickness, pain, or poverty, will refine and strengthen us, leading us to a bright, glorious reunion with our Savior.

A Day in My Life 4

Background: A year had passed since my father's death. I was living in Zababdeh, near Jenin, and teaching at the Arab American University. I had just received the scholarship to Turkey and was planning to leave for Turkey at the end of the month.

I decided to come home to visit this weekend. I wanted to come last week, but my mom and sister convinced me otherwise. I was so bored in my little apartment in Zababdeh that weekend. There is nothing to do in that small town. Last weekend I sat at home staring at four walls. There was nothing to watch on TV either. So, this weekend I said to myself, "I have to go home!!"

After hearing the news that said that the "closure is being lessened," I thought, *The trip home won't be bad.* The fifty-five-mile trip from Zababdeh to Beit Sahour should not take more than the usual three hours. In the past it would take me an average of four hours to go home during weekends to visit my mother in Beit Sahour. I tried to find a taxi to take me to the Qalandia checkpoint (near Ramallah). All the taxi drivers said that the checkpoint at "Alhamra" outside Jenin was not letting anyone out of the area. They said that even those with permits were getting turned back. I was also told that the alternative checkpoint "Altayaseer" was permanently closed. That left me waiting for a taxi driver who was willing to try other routes (dirt roads and hills and similar detours).

I waited about two and a half hours at the university until Zuhair came. Zuhair is a taxi driver that I usually ride with. He said he would take me with him even though I would be the ninth person in an eight-passenger van. Before we left, Zuhair gave me the spare key to his car to put in my bag. He said that sometimes the soldiers take his car key because he was sneaking people around the checkpoints. He wanted to hide the spare one because they would search him and the car until they found it and take the spare one too. By giving it to me, he would be sure that if the soldiers took his car key and left, he would be able to still go home.

We took off, taking a back road through Tulkarem. However, because there was a curfew on Tulkarem, we ended up taking a dirt road to avoid being seen. Anyone seen on the street during curfew is shot or arrested. I don't know if I can possibly explain what I mean when I say "dirt road." It is basically not a road meant for cars. It is merely a path on a hill between olive trees and rocks. We drove on this so-called road for half an hour. While inside this small van, I felt I was inside a box that a child was carrying and shaking. Our bodies were basically bumping on the sides and top of the car all the way. Of course the dust is a different story. I could not breathe all the way. People wonder why we Palestinians have the largest percentage of cancer patients—it must be all the dust we inhale.

Anyway, after driving on this road for half an hour, we saw soldiers in the distance. We had to back up all the way to where we came from. We had to drive it in reverse because there was no place to make a U-turn. When we came close to some Palestinians sitting in their backyard, we asked them for an alternate route. They told us there is another hill we can try to drive on, so we were off again; yet another dirt road—or path. We drove on this one, which was worse than the first. Shortly after we started we hit a dead end!! Disappointed, we knew we had to go back. There was another taxi with us, so both taxis would drive down different paths and whoever found an open road would call the other. We drove on the hill for over an hour. Sometimes we had to get out of the taxi so that it would be lighter and the rocks would not scrape the bottom of the taxi too much. Sometimes the taxi was driving over the rocks at a 90-degree angle with the ground, and I thought we would flip over! Finally, we got to a road that did not dead end. It went on and on, until it led us into a paved road. We were all thrilled.

We drove for ten minutes on that road when we were stopped by a checkpoint. The soldiers asked us to get out of the car. They searched all of our luggage, then took our identity cards to check them. We waited for them to return our identity cards for over an hour. Those in the car were fasting (due to the holy month of Ramadan for the Muslims). Muslims fast from sunrise to sunset. Now the sun was setting and they could not eat. As we were waiting at the checkpoint, I watched the people with me in the taxi smile, listen to music, and joke about the whole situation. After all they have been through, here they are hungry and tired, yet they manage to smile and not get frustrated with the whole situation. One of the guys with us gathered up enough courage to go and ask the solider if he would let them go to a nearby village and buy some food to break their fast. The soldier immediately shook his head, saying, "No."

We finally got our identity cards back and left that checkpoint. We got to another checkpoint. There were many people that were stopped at that checkpoint. The soldier stopped us and started yelling at the driver. He said he was not supposed to come this way. The soldier was pretty upset and for a moment I thought he would make us go back, but he let us through.

Fifteen minutes later we arrived at the Za'atara checkpoint. We stopped and the soldier demanded we get out of the car. We stood by the side of the taxi while the soldier searched all the bags. He took all the stuff from the bags and put it on the ground (all our clothes on the dirty road), then he threw the bags on the ground as well. After that, he started to search the taxi. He made the driver unscrew part of the engine to find out if something was hidden in there. He said that there are no curtains allowed in the car, so he took his knife and tore up all the curtains in the taxi. I found out later that we were lucky since the soldiers tore up all the seats in other taxis. All through the search the soldier would look at us and demand we stand "there" or move to "here" or to "not go there." After all this search, they said we can go.

We made it to the Qalandia checkpoint when it was already dark. Zuhair made sure I found a taxi to take me the rest of the way towards Beit Sahour. Zuhair was so nice. I felt so bad handing him 50 shekels, or about $12, for the fare—like he asked. With all he's been through, I feel if I give him $1,000 it won't be enough.

Barrier
Checkpoint
Israeli Settlement
AREA (A)
AREA (B)
Nature Reserve

MEDITERRANEAN SEA

Jenin

WEST BANK

Tulkarm

Tubas

Qalqiliya

Nablus

Salfit

Jordan River

JORDAN

Green Line

Ramallah

Jericho

Jerusalem

ISRAEL

Bethlehem

Green Line

WEST BANK

DEAD SEA

H2
Hebron

0   5   10
          Kilometers

I took a taxi to Abu Dis and from there to the Bethlehem checkpoint called the "Container." The taxi dropped me off at the checkpoint. There were no taxis there since it was now after 7:00 p.m. and the checkpoint was on a deserted, hilly road. The taxi driver that dropped me off wanted to make sure I got home safely, so he asked a truck driver to take me with him to Beit Sahour. The driver agreed. It was a truck carrying gas tubes. Another man coming from China with lots of suitcases got into the truck with us as well. The gas truck took me all the way to my door step. That ride was scary because I could smell the gas, yet the driver was smoking and was not concerned that he could blow us up at any minute.

The many people on the road that helped me get home were so sweet. When I got home, Zuhair, the taxi driver, called to check on me and see if I got home OK.

I got home and was about to pass out. My head felt like it was a time bomb ready to explode. It was probably the lack of food, the shaking, and the dust all together.

When I think about our life here I feel really grateful to be here. It is funny how many things become so insignificant when I watch what the people in Palestine go through. These people deal with checkpoints, dirt roads, arrests, and humiliation every day. One of the students with us in the taxi is from Jenin. Her name is Hanin. She said her brother was shot and killed at a checkpoint. Now, whenever she goes through checkpoints, her identity card is checked very carefully and she is harassed more than others. How I wish all the pain and suffering of my people would end, but there is nothing I can do about it. I know Heavenly Father is aware of us and loves every Palestinian, and He is in control. Someday, one of these days, it will all be made right.

Chapter 10

LIGHT

*"I am the light of the world: he that followeth me shall not walk
in darkness, but shall have the light of life" (John 8:12).*

"أَنَا هُوَ نُورُ ٱلْعَالَمِ. مَنْ يَتْبَعْنِي فَلَا يَمْشِي فِي ٱلظُّلْمَةِ بَلْ يَكُونُ لَهُ نُورُ
ٱلْحَيَاةِ." (يوحنا ٨: ١٢)

After my father passed away in 2003, I continued to teach at the Arab American University. The university encouraged faculty to seek higher education. The entire faculty in our Mathematics Department at the time had a PhD except me and one other teacher. I always had the desire to further my education.

All of my brothers pursued higher education. My brother Maher obtained a PhD in statistics from Indiana University. He returned to Palestine after graduating and started teaching at Bethlehem University. He taught there for twenty-five years. He actually taught me when I was a student at Bethlehem University. His passion and love for mathematics was contagious. Maher now teaches at the University of Dayton in Ohio.

Mazin is a lifelong learner. He obtained a PhD in zoology and then went on to get a degree in cytogenetics. He worked at Duke University and at Yale University. But his passion has always been animals. He enjoys spending time in nature, researching animals in Palestine, and helping the younger generation develop a love for nature by showing them the displays at the natural history museum he started in Bethlehem. Mazin wanted to continue the work of my uncle Sana Atallah, the first Palestinian zoologist, who died in a car accident in Iran before he realized his dream of starting a museum in Palestine.

My brother Walid is an accountant. He obtained his MBA and later became a CPA. He started his own accounting firm in Dallas, Texas.

Both my parents were teachers and worked, at times, as school principals. My mother was the principal of the girls' school that I attended as a child. My father was the principal of the boys' school (Al Masoudi) in Bethlehem. We have a family that has a passion for teaching. My sister Suhair is also a math teacher. So, five of us (my parents, Maher, Suhair, and me) are teachers. To some extent, we all have taught math, although my parents taught other subjects as well. My sister Samar wanted to become a teacher, but my parents encouraged her to become a nurse instead. It seemed like math and science were in our blood.

Because of the difficult situation in my country, many organizations offer scholarships to help Palestinians. Many in Palestine pursue higher education in other countries. Those scholarships are often competitive, because many people apply. My brothers pursued their educations in the United States. The salary my parents made in Palestine could not pay the tuition or expenses for my brothers. But they all obtained high grades in school and managed to get a scholarship or fellowship that made it possible for them to fund their own education.

I often thought about obtaining a doctorate degree. However, I was worried it would be too difficult, especially because it had now been many years since I had finished my master's degree at BYU. I had not applied for any scholarships, but the Arab American University was generous in providing opportunities for its faculty. One day, I received a letter saying that I had been granted a scholarship in Greece. However, I would have to go to language school and obtain acceptance to one of the universities there before I would be granted the scholarship. Learning a new language and going to a foreign country did not appeal to me. So, I declined the offer.

Only a month later, I received another offer. This one was for a scholarship in Turkey. I was accepted into a doctorate program in statistics at the Middle East Technical University in Ankara. I was more encouraged this time because the program was in English. They also told me that the scholarship would pay me 150 *million* Turkish liras a month. I felt I had won the jackpot! My joy did not last long, however—I soon found out that 150 million liras were equivalent to $100! Many told me that Turkey was cheap and that I could easily live on $100 a month (I discovered that this was far from the truth). This scholarship also required me to learn a new language, Turkish, for a year before I could start attending the university.

I was reluctant to waste a year of my life learning a language I might never use after my schooling. I also questioned the amount of money they were offering and didn't think it would be enough to support me. I decided to decline this scholarship offer as well. To my surprise, right after I called the scholarship committee and declined the offer, I felt I had made a terrible mistake. It didn't take me long to realize that the Holy Ghost was telling me that I needed to go to Turkey. Even though I didn't know the reason behind that prompting, I called back and told them that I had changed my mind and that I would gladly accept the scholarship offer.

I spent at least $700 a month living in Turkey, but somehow my small savings account never ran out. I found out why learning Turkish was essential. Very few people in Ankara spoke English, so it was hard to get by without knowing Turkish. The first two weeks in Turkey I was put in the girls' dorms in a room that was about twenty square feet and had seven other girls in it besides me. None of the girls spoke English or Arabic. It took me a whole day to find the bathroom, and it took me five days to find a phone. This is because communicating in sign language was not working. Leaving the dorms was scary because I knew I could not find my way back. I felt so alone and isolated.

After risking my life to attend church in Jerusalem, I thought I could handle anything that came my way. But I had never experienced something like this before. In Palestine, strangers helped me climb over walls and traverse fields to safely make it to church, where I knew I would find friends to encourage me. Here in Turkey, I was physically safe but had never felt so alone. No one could speak to me, and I could not understand anything going on around me. Without learning Turkish, I would continue to feel totally alone in this country. When I finally was able to find a phone and call my mom, she insisted that I come home. However, I knew I needed to be in Turkey and I did my best to learn Turkish once I started attending the language school.

I was thrilled to find the meeting place for the Ankara LDS branch. It was only a small group of members that met at the branch president's house, but it gave me a sense of belonging and was like a safe haven where I could actually communicate with people (many were American) who shared similar beliefs. One of the sisters in the branch offered me a room in her house to stay in. I was so relieved that I didn't have to stay in the dorm room anymore. After living in one room with seven other girls and having a locker as my closet, I felt I had moved from rags to riches.

Once I knew enough Turkish (actually, once I could say "hi" and "how are you?"), I became the official translator of the small branch. We had fewer than ten people in the branch when I started attending church there, but one of the families was a Turkish family who spoke no English. We were meeting in their country, but the church services had been con-ducted in English thus far. Even my broken Turkish and small attempts to translate for this family were met with gratitude and appreciation.

I commenced statistics classes at the Middle East Technical University only a few months after I arrived in Turkey. Learning Turkish was hard for me, but I discovered that once I knew the language, I could communicate with the people and learn about their culture. I initially thought that the Turkish people were cold, as they never spoke to me. But it turned out that it was only because they didn't feel comfortable speaking another language. I loved the Turkish people; they were warm, kind, and loving. I initially was reluctant to come and live in a Muslim country, but the Turkish people amazed me at how well they live their religion. They are honest and would serve others gladly. I had people walk with me to far places simply because they could not explain to me how to get to that place.

I enjoyed serving in multiple callings in the branch. Since there were very few members, I served in many callings at the same time (music coordinator, Sunday School teacher, Relief Society president, visiting teaching supervisor, and so on). We were part of a very small group of Christians in a Muslim country. In spite of that, we were welcomed and loved. We were not allowed to teach people and were very careful about even telling people that we were having church services. There are a few extremists in Turkey, and some explosions happened while I was there and two have happened since I left, killing many. Those who were killed were also Muslims. Unfortunately, extremists ruin the reputation of many Muslims, and that causes many to equate Islam with terrorism. This is similar to how a few extremists in Palestine are given attention in the media and therefore hurt the reputation of Palestinians. I wish the world could see the good side of Islam instead of focusing on the acts of a small group of Muslims who do such acts of terrorism. Since we could not teach the wonderful people in Turkey about the Savior, we felt that we had to teach by example and let our light shine.

I lived in the suburbs of Ankara, and it took me an hour by bus to get downtown, where the university was. Ankara is a very crowded city of six million people. The buses were often full, and I had to stand all the way, along with countless others who were also standing on the bus. It was a long and difficult trip, but having the quiet neighborhood, the trees, and the extra space at home made it worth the effort.

After I finished taking classes, I didn't have to go to the university very often. So I spent my time at home working on my dissertation. I worked with an amazing Indian professor, Moti L. Tiku, doing research on the Modified Maximum Likelihood Estimation Method. I really enjoyed living in Turkey and visiting the amazing places found there.

I was coming home from church one day in the summer of 2007. The bus was full, and it was hot. We were standing very close to each other, and I felt I would pass out. I was relieved to squeeze my way out of the crowded bus and take a breath of fresh air. As I walked the short distance from the bus stop to my apartment, I contemplated the lessons that were taught at church that day and felt gratitude for being in Turkey. Suddenly, a Turkish woman stopped me. I understood Turkish perfectly, but my spoken Turkish was not perfect. That is why I felt a bit uncomfortable when this complete stranger stopped me. She started to speak to me in Turkish and said, "I don't normally stop people on the street, nor do I normally talk to strangers, but I could not help but notice the light in your eyes." The woman proceeded to tell me about how her husband had left her and her children and how she was struggling financially and emotionally.

What was the light this woman saw in me? Where was that light coming from? Before I joined the Church, my world seemed dark for many years. I felt the powers of darkness around me. I felt helpless as I struggled with thoughts of despair and hopelessness. I felt lost and confused as I walked away from the light and stumbled in the darkness. It was hard for me to see where I was heading or to see any purpose for my life. You may have noticed that happening to you when you've walked out of a brightly lit room into a dark hallway. It is hard to see, and you may stumble. Walking toward the lit room, however, seems easy, and you can get there easily even if you are surrounded by darkness.

The Savior tells us, "I am the light of the world: he that followeth me shall not walk in darkness, but shall have the light of life" (John 8:12). As we walk toward our Savior, who is the Light of the World, things will become clearer. Also, as we follow Him, we will be able to reflect His light so that others can see His light radiating through us. Only light can dispel the darkness. In a dark world, we need to find light and hold on to it. Each of us can have that light within us. The Savior tells us, "Ye are the light of the world. . . . Let your light so shine before men, that they may see your good works, and glorify your Father which is in heaven" (Matthew 5:14, 16).

I especially noticed that light as I walked with Sister Ellett, who was

I am in the center, with Elder and Sister Ellett to my right.

serving a mission in Ankara with her husband. As Sister Ellett and I walked together, Turkish people on the street often stopped us. With a questioning look on their faces, they would ask, "Why does she glow like that? Tell us why she is so different." People noticed her light—or the Savior's light reflecting through this sweet sister.

The Ankara Branch is now growing fast and has almost eighty members. It started increasing when the first missionary couple arrived in Ankara—Elder and Sister Ellett. Now there are Turkish-speaking young missionaries in Turkey. I often help those missionaries practice Turkish as they Skype with me from the Provo MTC. I didn't want to learn this language initially, but I am honored that I can use Turkish to further the Lord's work and help missionaries bring the gospel to some of the amazing people I met in Turkey. The light of the gospel will illuminate countries that are currently closed to missionary work. The light of knowledge and truth is ever-needed all over the world.

Sometimes we feel the world is dark all around us and that light will never come. President Player, my district president in Palestine, taught me that sometimes we must be patient as we wait for the light. When I was discouraged one day and felt surrounded by darkness, I wanted to give up. What President Player told me at that moment stuck with me for many years. He reminded me of the First Vision and of Joseph Smith, a confused fourteen-year-old praying to know which church was true. These are Joseph's words:

"After I had retired to the place where I had previously designed to go, having looked around me, and finding myself alone, I kneeled down and began to offer up the desires of my heart to God. I had scarcely done so, when immediately I was seized upon by some power which entirely overcame me, and had such an astonishing influence over me as to bind my tongue so that I could not speak. Thick darkness gathered around me, and it seemed to me for a time as if I were doomed to sudden destruction.

"But, exerting all my powers to call upon God to deliver me out of the power of this enemy which had seized upon me, and at the very moment when I was ready to sink into despair and abandon myself to destruction—not to an imaginary ruin, but to the power of some actual being from the unseen world, who had such marvelous power as I had never before felt in any being—*just at this moment of great alarm, I saw a pillar of light exactly over my head, above the brightness of the sun, which descended gradually until it fell upon me.*

"It no sooner appeared than I found myself delivered from the enemy which held me bound. When the light rested upon me I saw two Personages, whose brightness and glory defy all description, standing above me in the air. One of them spake unto me, calling me by name and said, pointing to the other—*This is My Beloved Son. Hear Him!*" (Joseph Smith—History 1:15–18; emphasis added v. 17).

President Player then said, "Do you remember that First Vision and the darkness Joseph Smith felt and saw? Now remember the amazing light that followed!" It is true, oftentimes our days seem dark, but at the moments when we are about to give up because the darkness around us is so thick, light will come.

Elder Jeffrey R. Holland said, "Fighting through darkness and despair and pleading for the light is what opened up this dispensation. It is what keeps it going, and it is what will keep you going" ("Cast Not Away Therefore Your Confidence," BYU Devotional, March 2, 1999). When

I face times that are especially hard, I try to remember that there is light after darkness. There has never been a dark night that was not followed by a bright sunrise. Actually, throughout all of history, we know of only three nights that were not followed by the light of a glorious sunrise. Those were the days when the body of our Savior lay in the tomb. He is the Light of the World. If we follow Him, every dark night will be followed by a bright morning. The Savior is our hope, our light, our salvation, and our strength.

Lloyd Newell said: "When the darkness around us seems overwhelming, when we can't seem to find any light, it helps to remember that even when we can't see it, the sun is always shining. It may be hidden by the shadowy clouds of daily living, but it is always there. Perhaps night has made light seem like a distant memory, but darkness is ever the herald of dawn. No matter the darkness in our lives, the light of God's love still shines, and it can fill our hearts. It gives us hope in our suffering, joy in our sorrow, and light in our darkness. Yes, there is much in this life that brings sadness and distress. But God has also filled the world with an abundance of His light and love. If we seek it and receive it, this light can fill our lives" (*Music and the Spoken Word*, April 2017).

If you feel you have lost your way, or feel you are surrounded by darkness, I invite you to look for the Light of the World. He has always been there; He has never left your side. Turn to Him. Let Him hold your hand and lift you up. If you do so, your life will be filled with light. As you follow Him and obey His commandments, that light will become brighter and brighter until it has filled your entire soul.

Chapter 11

OBEDIENCE

"I would desire that ye should consider on the blessed and happy state of those that keep the commandments of God. For behold, they are blessed in all things, both temporal and spiritual" (Mosiah 2:41)

"أَرْجُو أَنْ تَتَأَمَّلُوا حَالَةَ بَرَكَةِ أُولَٰئِكَ الَّذِينَ حَفِظُوا وَصَايَا اللهِ وَسُرُورَهُمْ. لِأَنَّهُمْ مُبَارَكُونَ فِي كُلِّ الْأَشْيَاءِ سَوَاءً كَانَتْ زَمَنِيَّةً أَمْ رُوحِيَّةً" (موصايا ٢ : ٤١)

When I joined the Church, I had a desire to be obedient to all of Heavenly Father's commandments. I loved the Lord, and the Holy Ghost filled my soul with joy. I wanted to move away from sin and live a righteous life. When I lived in Utah, it seemed pretty easy to be obedient. Everyone around me went to church. On fast Sunday the cafeteria was closed, so it was easy to fast. Tea could not be found on BYU campus, so I had no problem obeying the Word of Wisdom. When I returned to Palestine, I found things to be very different.

I found opposition from my family and ridicule from my friends as I tried to obey the simplest commandments. My mother often told me to stop reading my scriptures and to not go to church. On fast Sabbath she would constantly try to get me to break my fast. I loved my mother dearly, but I felt my devotion to and my love for God were higher. I finally came to understand the words of the Savior in Matthew: "He that loveth father or mother more than me is not worthy of me: and he that loveth son or daughter more than me is not worthy of me" (Matthew 10:37). I constantly prayed for my mother's heart to be softened and for her to know that even though I put God first, I still loved her and respected her.

A commandment I thought would be easy to obey was attending church services. But due to the restrictions imposed on Palestinians, getting to the LDS branch, as I've described, was not such an easy task. The decision I made to continue to strive to be obedient no matter how hard things got strengthened my faith and solidified my testimony.

Each Sabbath posed extraordinary challenges that seriously deterred me from getting to and from church. Each week differed because I never knew what new roadblocks would be in place. Israeli soldiers closed small roads with piles of dirt or rock and placed checkpoints on the main roads. At first it was easy to avoid such checkpoints by climbing a nearby hill and hiding from the soldiers. Sometimes the taxi drivers would be willing to drive on dirt roads and fields that the soldiers had not blocked. But, as the restrictions increased and the separation wall started to be built, it became very difficult and dangerous to sneak into Jerusalem. A journal entry from one Sabbath in early November 2007 reminds me of my typical weekly expedition and all its complications.

I had just returned from Turkey after completing my PhD in statistics. At the time, the separation wall around Jerusalem was nearing completion. In 2002, Israel had started building this twenty-five-foot concrete wall to separate Palestinian cities, making it more difficult for Palestinians to enter Israeli areas. The wall, built on Palestinian land, surrounded our cities and even went through them. In the Palestinian city of Bethany, the wall cut the city right in the middle. That made it very difficult, if not impossible, for Palestinians to travel from one side of the city to the other. In Bethlehem, the wall went through the north end of the city, causing the busiest part of the city to become a ghost town. Some cities, such as Qalqilya, were surrounded completely, leaving only one entrance (usually a checkpoint) so the soldiers could monitor who goes in and out or close the city if they wish. Bethlehem was one of the lucky cities at the time because we had more than one way to exit the city (all monitored by checkpoints) and the wall blocked only the northern end.

However, leaving Bethlehem is one thing, and getting to Jerusalem is another. Beit Sahour, where I lived, was actually about five miles from Jerusalem. I remember that when I was a child, it took me fifteen minutes

A photo of me at the entrance of the Bethlehem checkpoint showing the separation wall.

to get there by bus. The bus fare was a mere shekel (about 25 cents). But things have changed since then. Now it takes about two or three hours to get to Jerusalem—that is, if I can manage to get through at all. It depended on the situation at the time and how many checkpoints I would find along the way. Luckily, that year, there was part of the separation wall near Qalandia (a city close to Ramallah north of Jerusalem) that was not completed yet. The incomplete part was a fence with a two-foot hole in it. The hole in the fence was about twenty miles away from Beit Sahour, but it took me an hour and a half to get there because I had to take the hilly back road to avoid Israeli checkpoints. I took a taxi to where the hole was and waited. I was with a group of Palestinians who also wanted to enter Jerusalem. We all waited for about half an hour until the soldiers on the other side of the hole left for a change of shifts. Only then could we go through the hole without being seen.

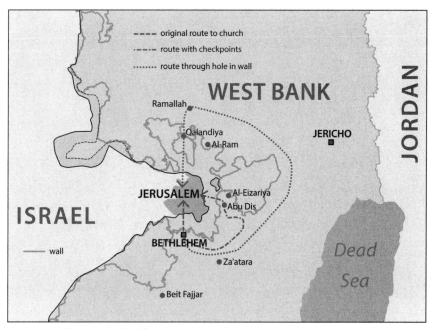

Bethlehem/Beit Sahour area map showing my route to Jerusalem before the wall, through the checkpoints, or using the back road.

I was thrilled to hear that the soldiers were gone. I could finally sneak through the hole and likely arrive at church on time. The difficulty of squeezing through the small hole did not discourage me, and neither did the muddy, rocky road that lay ahead. But only a few seconds after I had gone through the hole, I heard these words: "Don't move. The soldiers are coming!" A Palestinian man who was also trying to sneak through the hole said this as he took off running. With my heart pounding, I froze in place, unsure of what to do. Fences and walls surrounded me, and my shoes were stuck in the mud.

"Where should I hide?" I started to ask.

But he simply said, "Stay where you are; don't move." Just a few minutes earlier, this same Palestinian man had informed me that the Israeli soldiers were gone and that the way was clear to sneak through the small hole in the separation wall and enter Jerusalem. However, now

An example of a hole in the separation wall. The original hole I went through was much smaller.

this fellow Palestinian's words rang in my ears and made the possibility of getting caught or even shot by the soldiers very real.

I stood in place, breathless. Then suddenly I heard other voices say, "This way." I looked around me and realized that the voices were coming from behind a ten-foot concrete wall—another obstacle I needed to pass to get to church. This was the first wall that the Israelis had built to separate Ramallah from Jerusalem, before they had constructed the higher, twenty-five-foot wall. The original wall was left in place, now parallel to the higher wall, making more obstacles to cross. The only way past that ten-foot wall was to climb over it.

How do they expect me to climb this? I thought. With my body shaking in fear, I attempted to climb the wall, to no avail. The wall's surface was smooth cement, which gave me no foothold. Suddenly, I saw two hands clasped together by my feet and heard an urgent whisper: "Step up." Who was this man? And why did he help me, risking being arrested himself? I did not know the answer but sincerely muttered a thank you as I stepped on his hands. He lifted me up to catch hold of the top edge of the wall and climb over. Without hesitation, I made the ten-foot leap down the other side, conscious of the need to avoid wires and fences when I landed. I felt sincerely grateful that I wore pants to go to church that day.

Once on the other side, I joined other Palestinians who had also successfully crossed over the wall. We cautiously made our way to a hiding place, vigilantly watching the road for any sign of soldiers. When an Arab bus approached, we all jumped aboard with a prayer that the soldiers would not spot us. We could not ride in taxis or private cars in Jerusalem, because it is illegal for them to transport Palestinians from the West Bank. Taking an Arab bus was our only option.

I barely had time to find a seat on the bus, begin to catch my breath, and thank my Heavenly Father for His help when the bus driver looked back at us and said, "The soldiers at the checkpoint are motioning me to stop the bus. I'm sorry; it looks like you have been caught."

The two hours it had taken me to get this far from my home in Beit Sahour had all been for naught. I knew all too well what would happen next. The soldiers would either force me to return home or they would arrest me. I was emotionally and physically exhausted and was close to tears when the bus driver suddenly sped up instead of slowing down. He quickly drove the bus through the checkpoint while the soldiers were checking another car. I waited to hear gunshots fired at us or soldiers yelling, "Stop!" on the loudspeakers, but nothing happened. Without further incident, the bus reached Damascus Gate in Jerusalem, where I got off the bus and caught another bus that took me to the Mount of Olives next to the hill where the BYU Jerusalem Center is located. From there I walked the rest of the way.

The meeting at the Jerusalem Branch commenced at 10:00 a.m., and I had about a minute to clean the mud off my shoes and still be on time. Like most Sabbaths, my "commute" to church that day had taken close to three hours. But I was so grateful to be there, and I thanked Heavenly Father for His protection and enabling power. For years, He had helped me get to church amid similar dangerous and frightening circumstances;

Courtesy Chad Emmett.

BYU Jerusalem Center.

they were twelve of the most difficult and, at the same time, most joyful years of my life.

I feel I can relate to the experiences of Daniel in the Old Testament. The king made a decree "that whosoever shall ask a petition of any God or man for thirty days, save of thee, O king, he shall be cast into the den of lions" (Daniel 6:7). Daniel knew that the law of the land forbade him from praying. However, Daniel did not falter. He did not submit to the unjust law set forth by the king. Instead, Daniel "went into his house; and his windows being open in his chamber toward Jerusalem, he kneeled upon his knees three times a day, and prayed, and gave thanks before his God, as he did aforetime" (Daniel 6:10).

As a result of Daniel's obedience, the Lord protected him. When Daniel was cast into the den of lions, the Lord delivered him. The Lord had done the same for me. The law that Israel imposed on the Palestinians prevented me from being obedient to my God. That law prevented me from going to church to partake of the sacrament and be with fellow members of the Church. I knew God's laws were above any of man's laws. I knew that as I served and loved God and put Him first in my life, He would take care of me. I was protected not once, like Daniel, but many times as I strove to be obedient to His commandments.

For me, making that arduous and risky weekly trip into Jerusalem was more than an act of obedience. It was something I did because I felt my soul would simply die spiritually without it. Ever since I had joined the Church, I felt that I needed strength to obey the simplest commandments. Persecution from family members, literal roadblocks, and political turmoil often stood in the way of my obedience. However, day by day and one miracle at a time, I managed to persevere. President Russell M. Nelson said, "Keep *all* the commandments of God. . . . Obedience to the commandments of God will provide physical and spiritual protection. And remember, God's holy angels are ever on call to help us. . . . When we are faithful, He and His angels will help us" ("Face the Future with Faith," *Ensign,* May 2011).

I did feel protected and strengthened; however, this repeated weekly trip to church took a physical and emotional toll. One day after arriving at church exhausted, my friend asked me, "What happens if you get caught?"

"I don't know," I responded. "I never thought about it and never considered the possibility." I left Jerusalem after church that day on an Arab bus and headed to the Bethlehem checkpoint. It was always less stressful returning home because leaving Jerusalem was relatively easy. Most of the time, Palestinians aren't checked while entering Bethlehem. This return trip, however, would be different. I would soon find out what would happen if I got caught.

Shortly after the bus departed Damascas Gate, we noticed Israeli soldiers and police officers on the side of the road motioning for the bus to stop. My heart pounded in fear as a soldier, dressed in full military attire with his intimidating automatic rifle slung over his shoulder, entered the bus to check each passenger's identity card. What should I do? Should I lie and tell him I had lost my identity card so I wouldn't have to show him my green Palestinian card? I had often avoided lying to the soldiers even if it meant getting caught. As the soldier approached, I said a silent but fervent prayer. I was still shaking but felt prepared for whatever happened.

He stood in front of me with his hand extended. With trepidation, I reluctantly turned over my identity card. He looked at it and asked, "*Ween El Tasreekh?*" ("Where is the permit?"). Palestinians who live in the West Bank have green identity cards. Without a permit, a person with a green identity card is not allowed into Jerusalem. I told him honestly that I did not have the permit. In a loud voice, he commanded me to I get off the bus. Then he barked orders at me to stand by the side of the road and wait. Another Palestinian was already standing on the roadside. Speaking in Hebrew, the soldier demanded that the Palestinian man hand over his identity card. The man could not understand Hebrew, so the soldier said, "*Hawiya,*" which is the Arabic word for *identity card.* The man respectfully responded that he did not have his card with him. Raising his club and preparing to hit the man, the soldier again loudly demanded that the man hand over his identity card and proceeded to search the man and his things.

A few minutes later, Israeli police arrived. A police officer asked me in Hebrew what I was doing in Jerusalem. Even though I don't know Hebrew, over the years I have learned the basic "checkpoint language." For example, I know Hebrew sentences like, "Give me your identity card," or, "You are not allowed in," or, "What are you doing here?" So I understood what the officer was asking and told her in English that I had been in Jerusalem to attend church. She did not understand English and asked me to repeat my answer. I said the word *church* in English, and then in Arabic, and tried many methods to communicate, until she finally seemed to understand. However, her reaction—"Ah, OK"—did not indicate that she cared about the reason or what church meant to me or that I was clearly no threat to the peace of the city. Certainly others had used the same explanation after being caught, so coming to Jerusalem to pray was not deemed a legitimate reason to disobey laws.

After this initial interrogation, the police officer handed each of us, the man and me, a sheet of paper with information written in Hebrew and ordered us to sign it. I told her I couldn't sign something that I didn't understand. She said, "The form says that you have been found in

Jerusalem illegally, and you need to sign it." I did not want to sign it. The letter was two pages long, and I distrusted what was written on it and what I would unknowingly acknowledge by signing it. The Palestinian man beside me also refused to sign. The soldier grabbed his club and started to beat him, saying, "I will make you sign." The female police officer calmed the soldier down and told him to leave the man alone. Worried that this might happen to me and realizing I had no other options, I finally signed the paper.

We were both forced into the police car. I thought they were taking us to jail. I had no idea how I would explain this to my family and how I could be released. In the backseat, the man was still arguing with the soldier, which only made the soldier more violent. I kept praying that the man would just sign the form because I believed the soldier would seriously harm him. I prayed for the safety of that man and that, by some great miracle, we would not be arrested.

I knew my prayer was answered when the police car turned toward Bethlehem. Stopping at the Bethlehem checkpoint, they let us out and drove away. I was almost in tears, my heart full of gratitude. I finally felt safe in my own territory. The other man then asked me, "How did you manage to enter Jerusalem today?" After telling him about my horrible day, going through the hole, climbing walls, running in the mud, and hiding from soldiers, he said, "Did you walk much?" I told him that I didn't do much walking and took a taxi to where the hole was. He had a big smile on his face and replied, "Really? I had to walk three hours this morning on hills and mountains to get to Jerusalem. Tell me where the hole is. I am going right now."

Almost doubting my ears, I asked, "You are going there now? You are going to turn around and go back to Jerusalem after what you have been through?"

When he responded in the affirmative, I had no other choice but to explain to him where the hole was and how to get there. He went on his way, eager to get back on the road.

I often felt Heavenly Father's hands carrying me to and from church.

I was shot at once when the soldiers discovered me climbing a hill trying to sneak into Jerusalem. I was attacked twice by men who tried to rape me as I was alone on those hills. Somehow in both situations, the men didn't harm me. I had often wondered what prevented them and can only attribute it to the hand of the Lord and His protection. I seemed to have become invisible to the soldiers, because others would often be stopped while I was allowed to continue to walk.

However, getting caught that day was simply too much for me to handle. I was discouraged and started to fear that if I were caught another time, I wouldn't be released with a simple warning. I had heard people say that the first time you are caught you receive a stern warning, but the second time you will be arrested and imprisoned. I questioned whether I should ever try to go to church again. After years of facing these obstacles, I felt exhausted and drained.

Every day that following week, I knelt and pled to Heavenly Father for help. I told Him that even though I had promised that I would try to go to church each week, I simply could not do it anymore. I was emotionally and physically spent. I told Heavenly Father that I wanted Him to make it easier for me to go to church. Heavenly Father has always answered my prayers. Sometimes His answers came later than I wanted or not in the way I wanted, but my prayers to Him have always been answered. This time, however, I was praying for something that seemed impossible. In my mind, for Heavenly Father to answer this prayer, He would have to remove the restrictions, the wall, and the checkpoints, and I didn't see how that could ever happen. I wondered if, this time, He would choose to answer me by giving me greater strength to bear my burdens and the courage to sneak into Jerusalem as He had done in the past.

I did not perceive an answer to my prayer right away. Actually, the answer didn't come for a year. In the meantime, in place of going to the Jerusalem Center for church, I tried to create my own weekly worship service with prayer and scripture study in my home. I longed for the spiritual nourishment I had had at church, and I longed to partake of the sacrament. I thought I could keep my faith strong if I studied and prayed, but

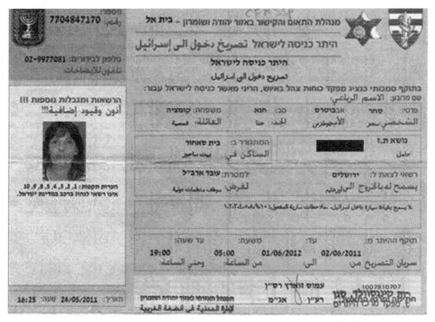

Israeli permit issued to me through my job with the United Nations.

it was really difficult. I had great members of the Church who would try to visit teach me every month, and I loved those visits. The message they gave me was the only gospel lesson I got each month, and oh, did I love it!

A year after that day of being stopped and almost arrested, an answer to my prayers finally came. I was offered a job with the United Nations Relief and Works Agency (UNRWA) in Jerusalem. Because the job was stationed in Jerusalem, UNRWA could secure a permit for me to enter the city legally. In December 2008, I finally received that blessed permit. This small piece of paper allowed me to be in Jerusalem from 5:00 a.m. until 7:00 p.m. every day. But the permit offered even more to me. Because I worked for the UN, I was granted a special permit to enter Jerusalem through any checkpoint around the city. Almost all other permits allow the bearers access only through the main checkpoint. Bethlehem's main checkpoint had a high volume of people wanting to pass through. During work days, the wait times could be as long as three hours.

I felt it a great privilege to again be able to enter Jerusalem, the city

Courtesy Joshua Hough.

Lines at the Bethlehem checkpoint during a normal workday.

of my birth, without restrictions. Thanks to that permit, I could now go to church through any checkpoint, show my permit, and catch a bus on the other side of the checkpoint. The trip to cover those five miles from Beit Sahour to the BYU Jerusalem Center would take half the time— about an hour and a half—and I would have no fear of being caught while walking by soldiers when I was in the Old City.

God had answered my prayers. No, the walls had not come down, and the checkpoints had not been removed, but I was able to cross them and go to church without fear. I felt my prayers had been miraculously answered, and I thanked Heavenly Father for His help. However, the blessings of my obedience did not stop there.

I thought getting that permit to enter Jerusalem in 2008 was the answer to my prayer, but it was only a small part of it. The Lord had something bigger and more wonderful in mind for me. His miraculous answer included establishing an LDS branch close to my home, where I could attend church freely and include other members who hadn't been to church in years.

Elder Joseph B. Wirthlin said, "The Lord compensates the faithful for every loss. . . . Every tear today will eventually be returned a hundred-fold with tears of rejoicing and gratitude" ("Come What May and Love it," *Ensign,* November 2008).

I believe that if we are obedient and have faith in Jesus Christ, we will receive such blessings—blessings that our minds cannot comprehend or imagine. I know this because that is what happened to me. I was blessed exceedingly, not only at the end of those twelve challenging years, but during those years when I faced dangerous conditions every week to get to church. When I look back on those hard years, when I was so alone, when my family tried to persuade me to leave the Church, and when getting to church took three hours, I think, in many ways, they were the happiest years of my life. The reason is that I had the Holy Ghost with me as my constant companion.

Sister Eliza R. Snow said: "When you are filled with the Spirit of God, and the Holy Ghost rests upon you . . . do you have any trials? I do not think you do. For that satisfies and fills up every longing of the human heart, and fills up every vacuum. When I am filled with that Spirit my soul is satisfied, and I can say in good earnest, that the trifling things of the day do not seem to stand in my way at all. . . . Is it not our privilege to so live that we can have this constantly flowing into our souls?" ("An Address by Miss Eliza R. Snow," *Latter-Day Saints' Millennial Star,* 36, no. 2 [1874]: 18).

King Benjamin tells us in the Book of Mormon, "I would desire that ye should consider on the blessed and happy state of those that keep the commandments of God. For behold, they are blessed in all things, both temporal and spiritual; and if they hold out faithful to the end they are received into heaven, that thereby they may dwell with God in a state of never-ending happiness. O remember, remember that these things are true, for the Lord God hath spoken it" (Mosiah 2:41).

I think the reason we find happiness when we obey is because we receive strength and comfort from the Holy Ghost. I did not have much support from my family and those around me, but my Heavenly

*Me waiting in line at a checkpoint on the way
to church after obtaining the permit.*

Me at the BYU Jerusalem Center.

Father was always there lifting me, strengthening me, and surrounding me with His spirit. The Holy Ghost guided me to the path I should take each week as I traveled the difficult road to church. He gave me an inner strength that I didn't think I had.

The blessings that I received because of my obedience didn't come right away; they came years later. Heavenly Father wants us to be obedient even when things are difficult. We should always show our devotion and love to Him by submitting our will to His and serving His children every day of our lives.

Chapter 12

DEVOTION

"By small and simple things are great things brought to pass" (Alma 37:6).

"إِنَّ الصَّغَائِرَ تَسْتَجْلِبُ الْعَظَائِمَ" (ألما ٣٧ : ٦)

The organization I started working for in 2008, UNRWA, was established to help Palestinian refugees in Lebanon, Syria, Jordan, and Palestine. There are over five million Palestinian refugees scattered all over the world, the majority of whom live in these countries. Those refugees were either driven out of or fled their homes during the wars of 1948 and 1967. They were never allowed back. Most of those refugees still carry their house keys, hoping to return to their villages and homes one day. I have family members who are refugees. My uncle's family used to live in Ramleh. During the Second World War, they sought refuge in Jordan until the war stopped. When they attempted to go back home after the war, they were not allowed in. Their house had been taken over by some Jewish settlers who had come from another country to reside in the newly established Israeli State. My uncle and his family, along with another uncle and cousins, have lost their right to live in Palestine. The refugee issue is at the core of the Palestinian/Israeli conflict. A Palestinian who grew up in Palestine and whose family has lived there for generations is not allowed to live there now, but a Jew who has never set foot in

Palestine has automatic citizenship and can come to Palestine and reside on Palestinian land.

My job as a data analyst at UNRWA involved analyzing the data we collected, assessing the needs of the Palestinian refugees, and providing them with the assistance they needed. After more than a decade of sneaking into Jerusalem to go to church, I now had a permit to enter and was able to regularly attend church meetings. At the time, there were three branches of the church in Palestine/Israel: one in Tel Aviv, one in Galilee, and one in Jerusalem. The Jerusalem branch is mainly composed of BYU students and faculty with a small number of people who are in Jerusalem for work and a few local members.

A short time after I started regularly attending church, President Okiishi, the branch president of the Jerusalem Branch, invited me to speak to him. Through tears, he told me that the Lord had called me to serve as the Relief Society president of the Jerusalem Branch. He said he had never felt such a powerful witness from the Spirit that this was the person the Lord had chosen for this calling. The assignment of Relief Society president afforded me the blessing of working with all the women in the branch, visiting them, and assisting them with their challenges. Being the Relief Society president in the Jerusalem branch had some challenges. We had new BYU students every semester. So we had to restructure Relief Society and make new callings every four months. It was a hard calling, but I loved it! We had amazing sisters in the branch, and I learned so much from them.

I discovered that there were actually a few members of the Church in Bethlehem, who, like me, had joined the Church in other countries. In branch council meetings we discussed how we could help these members. Because I knew how difficult it was for me to get to church, I yearned to help those members receive the blessings I had. The walls and restrictions were not going to be removed anytime soon, so we needed a more practical solution. The only viable answer to assist and strengthen them became clear: we would bring the Church to them. It was decided that

Bethlehem church building (sacrament meeting room).

we could start having sacrament meetings in Bethlehem at the home of one of the members.

The result was a simple meeting where local members could partake of the sacrament and participate in a lesson. Brother Whipple, from the Jerusalem Branch, was called to organize those meetings in Bethlehem. It was an amazing experience, and I felt the Spirit often as we met every week together to worship the Lord. We had a brief sacrament meeting followed by a Sunday School lesson. Because of my good command of English and Arabic, I was assigned to give the Sunday School lesson every week. As the Relief Society president in the Jerusalem Branch, I continued to attend church there (where meetings were held on Saturday), but I also attended church in Bethlehem (where meetings were on Sunday).

I felt we had started something magnificent in Bethlehem. It seemed like Satan did not want our meetings in Bethlehem to continue. Every Palestinian member of the Church in the area felt opposition and had many trials. Some lost their jobs, some lost family members, and some got sick, but we kept moving forward, doing the best we could to serve the Lord. For me, the greatest blessing was knowing that if I were to lose my job with the UN, I would still have a place to partake of the sacrament.

About a year later, I helped secure an apartment that we rented as a church meeting place. I purchased furniture and arranged for the apartment to be painted and for carpet and curtains to be installed. Then with the help of some members, we cleaned the space to prepare it for church meetings. It felt so peaceful there. Finally, our own church building!

A short while later, we rented the adjacent apartment, which had a large room that could be used for our sacrament meetings. We now had separate rooms for Relief Society, Primary, priesthood quorums, and other meetings. I had my hands full taking care of the Bethlehem church building, teaching weekly lessons there, working in a very demanding job with the UN, and being the Jerusalem Branch Relief Society president. I remember that in August of 2011 I was especially overwhelmed. I felt I had no time left for my family and was constantly running around trying to get everything done. I hated to see the look on my mom's face as I got home every day later than expected. I finally decided to pray about my heavy commitments. I told Heavenly Father that I had too much to do and I could not handle it.

A week later, I received a call from my district president, President Player, who said he wanted to come over and visit me in my home. President Player said that the Lord wanted to extend a calling to me to serve as the district Relief Society president. Here I was complaining to the Lord that I had too much to do, and He responded, "Here, why don't you do this as well?" I simply did not know if I had more time to devote to this new calling. I told my district president that I wanted to think and pray about this call.

After he left, I went to my room and prayed. When I closed my prayer, I was directed to open my scriptures to the fifteenth chapter of John, where I read these words: "I am the vine, ye are the branches: He that abideth in me, and I in him, the same bringeth forth much fruit: for

Courtesy Kent Jackson.

Elder Rasband in the Bethlehem Branch sacrament meeting.

without me ye can do nothing" (John 15:5). I had a sweet confirmation that this calling actually had come from God and that with His help I could do what He was asking me to do.

In February 2012, almost two years after that first meeting in Bethlehem, an official Church group was organized there. A group is smaller than a branch, but it was still our own. It was amazing to hear our district president announce the formation of the Bethlehem group. I was the district Relief Society president at the time, and I soon learned that district leaders were also responsible for groups in the district. Thus, in addition to my calling as district Relief Society president, I was now the Relief Society and Primary president of this new small group. We worked with a group leader, who was also called. My counselor, Emily, was a great help in reaching out to the sisters. It was a big responsibility, but it was a privilege to serve the Saints in Palestine. Due to travel distances, another church group was organized in Ramallah, where Saints from the north could meet and have meetings.

That same month, Elder Ronald A. Rasband, then of the Seventy, visited Jerusalem. This was his first visit since the organization of the

Bethlehem group. Tony, one of the Palestinian members, approached him regarding the name of the Church district. Tony explained that it seemed strange that the Church would call it the "Israel District"—Palestinian members felt that the name disregarded them. Only days after that meeting with Elder Rasband, the Church changed the name of our district from the Israel District to the Jerusalem District.

Two years after the organization of the Bethlehem group, in 2014, our district president announced, through joyous tears, the organization of the Bethlehem Branch. The branch members consisted of all Palestinian members anywhere in the country. This meant combining the Ramallah and Bethlehem groups into one branch.

So, now, the Jerusalem District had four branches: Galilee, Tel Aviv, Jerusalem, and Bethlehem. Because of the travel restrictions that Israel imposed, Palestinians living anywhere in the West Bank, an area of over two thousand square miles, had to attend church in the Bethlehem Branch—even if they lived fifteen minutes away from one of the other Jerusalem District branches.

After the Bethlehem Branch was organized, I was called as the Primary president of that branch. The members of our Bethlehem Branch were scattered all over the country. And because of the separation wall and checkpoints, it took members a long time to travel to church. We had some members that lived two hours away, and some four hours. Those members were often the only LDS people in their towns. Visiting and home teaching was a challenge, especially since all members in our branch were poor and didn't own cars.

If you live in the West Bank, living your faith and keeping the commandments can be difficult. You are alone, and you are the only representative of the Church in your area. A lot depends on you. How you act, how you live, and what you choose to do every day matters.

"Oh, you don't drink coffee? Don't worry. We can make some tea instead," were words I often heard when I visited people in their homes. It is part of the Palestinian culture to serve coffee to guests. It is considered rude not to serve something (usually tea or coffee). I often had to explain to people that I didn't drink tea or coffee and would prefer not to drink Coke (that was usually the third option offered).

Growing up, I drank tea with my family at breakfast and dinner. This was our tradition. When I came home from BYU as a member of the Church, however, I had stopped drinking tea. I would drink herbal tea, milk, or something else. My family's reaction was often something like, "Do you think we will go to hell for drinking tea?" or, "Do you think God notices what you drink?" Even though I tried not to show it, their comments bothered me.

One day I was at my sister Suhair's house, and she had guests. She said, "If I make tea, Sahar won't be able to drink with us, so I am making herbal tea for everyone." It was a simple act, but it made me feel great inside. Over the years, my family's tea-drinking habits have changed; they drink it less and less. I have even heard more positive comments from them: "Sahar is so calm and happy. Maybe it is because she doesn't drink tea!"

Even though we can't teach the gospel in Palestine, our example is essential. We need to go out of our way to serve others and be a light in a dark world. In Palestine, we don't keep our faith; our faith keeps us going. Since we lack support from a strong Church organization and from strong Church members, our hearts and minds often turn to God. Heavenly Father is someone who is always there for us. I have been able to find strength and have often found support from the Lord during difficult times in my life. He has carried me, and I have felt His loving arms surround me.

My counselor Emily and I traveled for hours to visit various branches and members in the district. Sometimes our visiting teaching trips would take all day. There was a family in Tulkarem, a city in northern Palestine, who had little contact with the Church because they lived far from Bethlehem. The family members were the only Christians in their town, and even though they lived close to Tel Aviv, they were not allowed to go to church there due to the travel restrictions and checkpoints. It took me about four hours to get from Bethlehem to Tulkarem, picking Emily up on the way. The trip back was another four hours. That sweet family would always prepare a great meal for us. We were fed physically and spiritually as we visited with them and shared a gospel message.

I often felt the love that the Savior had for the people who lived in Palestine. I believe that because the Savior was in Palestine as a "missionary," He has a special love in His heart for the people that live there, regardless of their background or religion. I felt and saw His hand in the establishment of the Bethlehem Branch and in the work of the Church in Palestine.

Recently, I started putting together jigsaw puzzles in my free time. I have found that it helps me relax as I take my mind off other things and focus on completing the puzzle. Someone once gave me a few puzzles that she didn't want anymore. After my cousin and I finished putting together one of them, we discovered it was missing a single piece. I felt that my efforts were wasted. How could one piece out of five hundred pieces make such a difference? Well, it can, because the puzzle is not complete without it.

In life, each of us represents a piece of the puzzle. At first we don't quite know where we fit since we don't see the big picture. Heavenly Father guides us to where He wants us to labor. In my life, I have sometimes questioned why Heavenly Father asked me to go to a particular place or do a particular task. Heavenly Father has allowed me to step back and see the whole picture once or twice in my life. In those moments, I have been able to see why I was needed in that particular place at that particular time. Each of us is important and needed because without each of the pieces, the picture will never be complete.

When I felt impressed to return home after graduating from BYU, I wondered why Heavenly Father wanted me to go back to Palestine when I wanted so badly to stay in the United States. In Palestine, as I was sneaking into Jerusalem to get to church and facing all kinds of hardships living in a place of conflict, I still wondered, *Why am I here?* But now I thank my Father in Heaven for placing me in Palestine during those many hard years of my life. Those trials were exactly what I needed to grow and to develop the testimony that I now have. He has also shown me how my testimony can lift others, and I am eternally grateful for that.

I hope each of you knows how important you are in Heavenly Father's plan. Each of us is loved, and each one of us has a skill and ability that is unique. Without you and the piece you add, the picture will not be complete. I hope each of us can pray to know what Heavenly Father wants us to do, whose life He wants us to touch, whose knees He wants us to strengthen, and then go forth and act on those promptings—serving, loving, and lifting others. Sometimes the things He asks us to do may be difficult, but they will always be things that will bring us the highest degree of joy and peace.

Chapter 13

TRUST

"Trust in the Lord with all thine heart; and lean not unto thine own understanding. In all thy ways acknowledge him, and he shall direct thy paths" (Proverbs 3:5–6).

"تَوَكَّلْ عَلَى ٱلرَّبِّ بِكُلِّ قَلْبِكَ، وَعَلَى فَهْمِكَ لَا تَعْتَمِدْ. فِي كُلِّ طُرُقِكَ اَعْرِفْهُ، وَهُوَ يُقَوِّمُ سُبُلَكَ." (أمثال ٣: ٥–٦)

After my call to serve as the district Relief Society president in 2011, I finally felt that I was making a difference. I was visiting branches in the district, strengthening sisters, organizing district Relief Society conferences, teaching in the Bethlehem group, and taking care of my mother, who had been diagnosed with hepatitis C and was not doing well. I also felt needed at my job with UNRWA, which had become demanding because we were building a new database and I was in charge of all the quality control and monitoring all the data being collected. My job was a relatively high-paying job, and it provided me with the permit to enter Jerusalem. Without that permit I would not have been able to fulfill my calling as district Relief Society president, and I wouldn't be able to enter Jerusalem, my beloved birth city.

So when I received an impression from Heavenly Father to quit my job, I was shocked. *Quit my job?* It seemed like a crazy thing to do, especially without a backup job. However, that was the impression I had received after praying over and pondering my current circumstance. In addition to taking away my salary, quitting my job would reintroduce other challenges to my life.

I reasoned that it made no sense to quit a job without having another job lined up. I was on vacation in the United States at the time that I was considering this, and one of my friends suggested that I meet with Elder Bruce D. Porter of the Seventy and discuss my thoughts with him. I became good friends with the Porters while serving in my calling in the Jerusalem District. As I waited for my meeting with Elder Porter, I turned to the scriptures for connection with the Spirit and to possibly receive more direction. The scriptures fell open to Matthew 6, where I began reading: "Therefore I say unto you, Take no thought for your life, what ye shall eat, or what ye shall drink; nor yet for your body, what ye shall put on. Is not the life more than meat, and the body than raiment? Behold the fowls of the air: for they sow not, neither do they reap, nor gather into barns; yet your heavenly Father feedeth them. Are ye not much better than they?" (Matthew 6:25–26). Even though this passage shares counsel Jesus gave to His leading disciples, I felt I was directed to that scripture for a reason and that Heavenly Father wanted me to trust Him. But I also felt that my faith was too weak to do what He asked without knowing what the future held. When I met with Elder Porter, he gave me a blessing and said that I should trust the Lord and that many doors would open up to me if I obeyed the Lord's commandments.

Even though I told my boss about my intention to quit, I could not gather the courage to write an official letter of resignation. One day after church, I sat on the Mount of Olives and looked over the beautiful city of Jerusalem—a city that I had grown to love. I gazed over the hill to the right at Al-Maqasid Hospital, where I was born. Right in front of me was the holy mount with the beautiful Dome of the Rock within the amazing Old City walls, where the Temple of Herod stood when Jesus lived here. Just beyond the walls was the place where Christ was crucified and then buried in the Garden Tomb, a place that I absolutely loved. That empty tomb reminded me of the reality of the Resurrection and the power of the Atonement: "He is not here: for he is risen" (Matthew 28:6)! My heart almost stopped as I considered the possibility of never again being able to see these places that were so dear to my heart.

If I quit my job, my permit would be taken away, and I would return to the same restrictions most Palestinians lived under in the West Bank. Once more, I would be unable to enter Jerusalem, or Galilee, or Yafa, or many of the amazing places in my home country. My heart ached and my eyes filled with tears as I looked at the holy mount and gazed over the city walls of old Jerusalem. Palestinian Christians are sometimes given holiday permits during Christmas and Easter, which allow them to enter Jerusalem during holidays. Although such permits are rare, I knew that if I quit my job, I would somehow be able to return to the city in the future. As I thought of that possibility, I felt renewed hope, knowing that I was not saying goodbye to my beloved city forever.

It took me two months to finally quit my job. I started working only part-time for a couple of months. This made quitting easier and helped me still do what I needed to do at work. I finally officially turned in my resignation on the first day of September. I still had no idea what I would do after I quit, and my family thought I was crazy to leave such a good job.

Just a few days after I had submitted my resignation, I sat in my room reading the September 2012 *Ensign* (which actually had one of my articles in it, "Loving My Enemies"). As I read the first few articles in the *Ensign,* a clear impression came to my mind: "You should go on a mission." I shook the feeling away, thinking that it couldn't be real. But the feeling persisted and grew stronger. I had no desire to go on a mission and knew that my family would not be supportive of that decision. Going on a mission had never crossed my mind in the past. I knew that I had little money, and probably insufficient savings to finance a mission. But Heavenly Father was clearly telling me to go. I knelt down and prayed. Again, the instruction was clear—clearer than anything I had experienced since the day I prayed to know if I should be baptized.

I was in a state of shock for days. I did not tell anyone about this impression except my counselor and friend Emily. Incidentally, she told me she had received the same impression that I should serve a mission after reading the same *Ensign* article! I did not mention the idea to my family, especially because I couldn't just say: "I am going somewhere, but I don't know where, I don't know when, and I don't know what I will be doing. However, I feel I should go." I knew that it would be easier to tell my family after my actual mission call came.

On Monday, October 15, I felt in my heart that my call had been made. I received my mission call in the mail later that week. The news was shocking to say the least. I was called to the England London South Mission. I would serve in the mission office. I could not think of a more perfect place. My call said I would report to the mission office in England on January 28, 2013.

Telling my mother of my decision to leave home to serve a mission was especially hard because, of my whole family, my mother was the one who had never accepted my membership in the Church. She had also never given up on trying to convince me to leave it. Almost daily, she asked me, "Aren't you going to leave these Mormons?" or ,"When are you going to become smart and see that what you are doing is wrong?" or, "Do you really think your God notices when you fast?" or, "Are you ever going to stop this nonsense?" Despite her outward expressions, I knew my mother could see that joining the LDS Church had changed me for the better. She would never admit that to me, of course!

One day, I overheard her speaking to my brother on the phone. My niece had received a scholarship to BYU, and my brother was reluctant to send her there, fearing that she may end up joining the LDS Church like I had.

"Well, what if she becomes like Sahar and joins the Church?" he asked my mom.

My mother readily responded, "What is wrong with her joining the Church? Look at Sahar; she is great."

One morning, I finally gathered up the courage to tell my mother about my mission. I told her I was going to England to "volunteer" for a year. My mom took it better than I thought she would, with only a few complaints, and then she appeared to forget about it. I almost thought she was going to be okay with my decision to go. But then I realized that maybe she thought I was not serious about it. She had no idea that for weeks I had been working on this—preparing for it, having medical tests done, completing all the paperwork, and receiving an official call. Going back on my decision was not an option anymore.

Some days later she realized I was going ahead with my plans and started to become upset. She started quizzing me:

"Why don't you just go for one month?"

"Arrange a meeting for me with your leader! I want to talk to him."

"How much will they pay you?" (She asked this one more than once.)

"How will you live there, on what money?"

After seeing my mother struggle, I tried to tell her the real reason I was going. I said, "Mom, I know you don't believe in God, but I do, and I want you to know that He was the one who called me to go to England."

Her first comment was, "God would not ask you to leave your sick mother." Then, after thinking about it for a while, she said, "You must have met someone and are going to go marry him in London. Do you think I will believe that God told you to go? Whatever!"

A few weeks passed, and my mother saw that my determination to go had not changed. So she resorted to more drastic measures. One day she declared, "I am not going to eat until you change your mind and decide not to go to England." She did not eat breakfast and seemed serious about her hunger strike. I knew she was not serious, but I still worried. I left the house one day and then realized that I had forgotten my cell phone at home. I came back to pick it up and found my mother eating. She had waited for me to leave before she started eating so I wouldn't see her.

A week later she said, "That's it. I am going to kill myself if you go." Then she called my sister and asked her to buy some "mouse poison" from the pharmacy so she could drink it and commit suicide.

This went on for a few days, refusing to eat and acting like she wanted to kill herself. But she calmed down, and I noticed that she was eating again and feeling better. I said, "Mom, do you still want to kill yourself?"

She said, "No, I decided there are a lot of things I still want to do in my life."

I write all of this with a smile on my face because I know my mother and I know she was not serious about any of the things she said. I knew she loved me and wanted what was best for me. All she wanted was for me to stay and not go to England. I know it was hard for her to see me go. With her hepatitis C and diabetes, my mother's health was declining. That is why it was very difficult for me to leave her, but I knew she would be protected and blessed.

I left for England in January. Since it was very clear to me that Heavenly Father wanted me to be in England, I thought that I would make a big difference, teach many people, and bring others into the Church. That didn't happen. And yet, my time in England was amazing. I loved being surrounded by missionaries all day, every day. That was different and new for me. At home I was the only member of the Church and was always surrounded by nonmembers. I felt my mission was a break from the harsh world I had been living in—a vacation from all the hardships, checkpoints, turmoil, and persecution. I felt Heavenly Father's presence and His love constantly, and I felt my soul was nourished. The enthusiasm and eagerness of the young missionaries in England were amazing. Their examples gave me strength and increased my faith.

I still don't know why the Lord called me on a mission, but I know He knows. I trust that someday I will know why I needed to be in England at that particular time. But even if I never find out, it does not matter. I know Heavenly Father loves me so much and will always do what is best for me.

Through the whole process of my mission, I learned to trust the Lord. I learned that sometimes we are asked to do things that don't make sense, like quitting our job or leaving our families. However, I know that whatever path Heavenly Father asks us to travel will lead us to happiness and will bring us closer to Him. I often feel that my life is like a big maze. Getting from the start of a maze to the end is easy if you can see the whole picture. However, in my life, there have been times when I have not been able to see the whole picture. When I stand at a crossroads and Heavenly Father asks me to go in one direction, I sometimes feel reluctant, especially if I notice rocks, hills, and uncertainty along that path. My life has taught me that the path He chooses for me will always lead me to happiness and fulfillment, no matter what it looks like at the start. As I have traveled the paths that He has set for me, I have never traveled them alone. My Savior, Jesus Christ, knows the way. He is the way. He has traveled those paths and knows every rock and every hill. He has often traveled with me through every step and has been there to comfort and strengthen me.

When I taught at the Arab American University and lived in Zababdeh, I had a neighbor who was a shepherd. Each morning, he would take his sheep out to the fields. His sheep followed him, sticking close together. One day, the shepherd forgot something and had to go home to get it. He left his sheep by my house and went back home. The sheep stood still and waited for the return of their shepherd. There was a field full of long, green grass by the side of the road, but the sheep did not go there. They waited patiently for their shepherd to return. They trusted that their shepherd would lead them to a much better place.

Our Savior is the Good Shepherd, and if we trust Him, He will lead us to green fields, where we will find happiness and peace. As tempting as the grass may seem on the side of the road, I know that if I keep my eyes on my Shepherd and follow Him always, I will be fed spiritually and physically.

"The Lord is my shepherd; I shall not want. He maketh me to lie down in green pastures: he leadeth me beside the still waters. He restoreth my soul: he leadeth me in the paths of righteousness for his name's sake. Yea, though I walk through the valley of the shadow of death, I will fear no evil: for thou art with me; thy rod and thy staff they comfort me. Thou preparest a table before me in the presence of mine enemies:

On my mission in front of the London England Temple. Left to right: my missionary companion Sister Hess, me, and Sulaiman (a brother who came from Jordan to receive his own endowment and get sealed to his wife and parents).

thou anointest my head with oil; my cup runneth over. Surely goodness and mercy shall follow me all the days of my life: and I will dwell in the house of the Lord for ever" (Psalm 23).

We are all trying to find our way back home to Heavenly Father, but we don't always know which path to take because we cannot see the whole picture. In life's maze, you have to trust that the Lord will lead you to the right path. The Savior not only directs you, but He walks with you. He knows the path, for He traveled it once before. Describing Himself, the Lord tells us, "I am the way, the truth, and the life" (John 14:6).

Chapter 14

GRATITUDE

"I have learned, in whatsoever state I am, therewith
to be content" (Philippians 4: 11).

"قَدْ تَعَلَّمْتُ أَنْ أَكُونَ مُكْتَفِيًا بِمَا أَنَا فِيهِ." (الرسالة إلى أهل فيلبي ٤: ١١)

I sat by a Muslim woman on the bus one day. She carried a big bundle of grape leaves and was heading to Jerusalem to sell them. One of the famous dishes back home is stuffed grape leaves. We call it *warak dawali*. We stuff the leaves with rice and meat. This sweet lady told me how the soldiers had blocked her way to her grapevine field and how she had to sneak by the soldiers at night to pick those leaves. She would later carry that bundle on her head and go around the checkpoint through the back road so that the soldiers didn't make her turn back. She had paid what was equivalent to one and a half dollars for the bus, and would have to pay one and a half dollars on the way back, too. She also had to pay about a dollar as a bus fare for the big bundle of grape leaves! She would sell her grape leaves in Jerusalem for about twenty-five cents a pound, making very little money. Yet she was grateful—grateful that she was able to pick her leaves without getting caught and that she was finally going to sell them.

I am enormously blessed. I am blessed with my knowledge of the gospel and the plan of salvation. I am blessed to know that I have a

Courtesy Luis Astudillo C./Andes News Agency.

Some of the destroyed houses in Gaza.

Father in Heaven who loves me. I can't begin to thank Him for changing my heart and filling me with His spirit. My life has taught me to trust Him. I know He would never allow anything bad to happen to me. All the trials and hardships I went through were put in my way for a reason. Without them, I would not be the person I am now.

When I was a child, I used to compare myself to others. For example, every time my cousin bought something, I would ask, "Why don't I have that too?" Recently I started again comparing myself to others but thought, *Why don't they have what I have?*

My cousin Rana had the chance to visit Gaza while she was working with World Vision. Rana was shocked that the people in Gaza seemed happy and grateful. They are poor, they are not allowed to leave Gaza, many have lost their homes (over 350,000 of them are homeless), they have no electricity most of the day, and they have little access to clean water, but they were grateful for what little they had. Almost every family has been affected by Israeli attacks and has lost homes or family members. A member of our Bethlehem Branch, Dima, lost her aunt in Gaza.

When an Israeli missile hit her uncle's house, Dima's aunt died and her cousin lost most of his limbs. Dima's grandparents' house in Gaza was also bombed, but luckily no one was harmed.

Elder Richard G. Scott said: "In this uncertain world, there are some things that never change: the perfect love of our Heavenly Father for each of us; the assurance that He is there and will always hear us; the existence of absolute, unchanging truths; the fact that there is a plan of happiness; the assurance that success in life is attained through faith in Jesus Christ and obedience to His teachings because of the redemptive power of His Atonement; the certainty of life after death; the reality that our condition there is set by how we live here. A strong testimony gives peace, comfort, and assurance. It generates the conviction that as the teachings of the Savior are consistently obeyed, life will be beautiful, the future secure, and there will be capacity to overcome the challenges that cross our path" ("The Power of a Strong Testimony," *Ensign,* November 2001).

After I returned home from my mission in 2014, I searched for a job for month after month. Nine months passed and my savings started to run low. I could not understand why Heavenly Father did not provide me with a job after I had been obedient in serving Him and had offered many fervent prayers. After nine months of unemployment, a friend of mine offered me a job in New York as a secretary in his office. He said I had to go to New York for a week, take and pass an exam, and then go back home to obtain my work visa. I was reluctant to take a job with low pay, but I was grateful for the possibility of having a job. I booked a round-trip ticket to New York in September of 2014. After receiving the test results, I was shocked to discover that I had failed. That job as a secretary was not a possibility anymore. I questioned why Heavenly Father would close the only door I felt I had to support myself. I had spent a lot of money on the plane ticket, and it was all in vain.

Knowing that I was not able to find work in Palestine, I decided to stay in the US and try to find work there. I canceled my return ticket even though it was nonrefundable. My chances seemed slim because in order to get a job in the United States, I must have authorization to work, and in order to get that authorization to work I must have a job first. After searching for months, I finally gave up hope of finding work in America. I used the remaining money I had to book a one-way flight home. Only a few days before my flight, I had a job interview with BYU–Idaho. Acting in faith, I again canceled my ticket home and decided to stay in the United States. I was offered the job at BYU–Idaho, and I now teach in the mathematics department there. I signed my contract with BYU–I on March 13, 2015—one day before my tourist visa expired. As I look back at those events, I realize they were all planned, not by me, but by my Father in Heaven.

I became upset when I didn't get the job in New York, but if I had, I would be working there as a secretary instead of teaching at this amazing university. Heavenly Father knew the time had to be right for me to be here. He knew when and how to make things happen. I just needed to trust Him. We sometimes ask for things and wonder why Heavenly Father does not grant them. Well, oftentimes it is because He wants to give us something better. Something so magnificent that we don't dare ask for.

The Lord tells us: "Verily, verily, I say unto you, ye are little children, and ye have not yet understood how great blessings the Father hath in his own hands and prepared for you; and ye cannot bear all things now; nevertheless, be of good cheer, for I will lead you along. The kingdom is yours and the blessings thereof are yours, and the riches of eternity are yours. And he who receiveth all things with thankfulness shall be made glorious; and the things of this earth shall be added unto him, even an hundred fold, yea, more" (D&C 78:17–19).

Throughout my life, I have seen myself as though I were the driver, with the Savior sitting beside me in the passenger seat. He has been able to advise me on which path to take and warn me when rocky roads were coming ahead. He has also been able to comfort and strengthen me when driving was especially stressful or even dangerous. It was not until my mission that I found myself moving over to the passenger seat and letting the Savior take the wheel. I was able to see His hand in my life in ways that I had never seen before. I realized that He knew all the details of my life and He cared about me.

I am a person who likes to be in control. But I have come to realize that when the Lord plans the trip and drives, it is a much smoother ride. I have discovered that submitting my will to His is the only way to true happiness and peace. I strive to align my will to the will of the Lord, and I know that His will is always the best for me.

Chapter 15

PEACE

"Peace I leave with you, my peace I give unto you: not as the world giveth, give I unto you. Let not your heart be troubled, neither let it be afraid" (John 14:27).

"سَلَامًا أَتْرُكُ لَكُمْ. سَلَامِي أُعْطِيكُمْ. لَيْسَ كَمَا يُعْطِي ٱلْعَالَمُ أُعْطِيكُمْ أَنَا. لَا تَضْطَرِبْ قُلُوبُكُمْ وَلَا تَرْهَبْ." (يوحنا ١٤ : ٢٧)

Jerusalem, the city of my birth, means "City of Peace." My parents were actually going to call me Salam, which means "peace" in Arabic. Instead, I was given the name Sahar, which means "awakening" or "dawn" (the end of the night and the first ray of sun). Peace was a feeling that was foreign to me and that I grew up wondering about. I had heard many speak about it, but for the first twenty-four years of my life, I didn't know what peace was.

My young life overflowed with sounds of rifles, long days of curfew, the agony of smelling tear gas, house demolitions, arrests, and injustices. I shivered in fear one day as my friends and I hid behind a fence when an Israeli settler got out of her car and started shooting at us. I was fourteen years old and we had been playing in the street at the time. Luckily, we managed to run and hide behind that fence. But as I sat behind the fence, I had the feeling that the bullets would penetrate the fence and slice through my young body. I hated guns and the sound of gunshots. There was pain every time I heard that sound, and I heard it often.

I remember being awakened in the middle of the night as a young girl to hear that my neighbors' house was about to be demolished by the Israeli soldiers. My neighbors' son had been caught in a demonstration against the occupation. Demolishing his house was the punishment. Our family and other neighbors gathered to give support to this family, even though the time was approaching midnight. The soldiers knocked at their door and gave them only a few minutes to take out a few belongings before blasting down their two-story house, leaving them homeless. Shock and disbelief covered their faces as they quickly piled their belongings in the yard. *What would I have taken if I was given only minutes to gather my things?* I thought.

Growing up, I felt shaken up by every event. It was emphasized to me again and again that peace was something that could not be established. During my teenage years, I saw many young men get killed. One particular young man, seventeen-year old Hazim, was killed in my town. Hazim died when an Israeli dumdum bullet hit him in the side. Dumdum bullets explode upon impact, making it almost impossible to save a person hit by one. Dumdum bullets are internationally banned, but that did not stop the Israeli soldiers from using them on Palestinians. After being shot by that dumdum bullet, Hazim ran a few feet and died in the arms of my ten-year-old niece, Lina, who was playing with her friends nearby. When I visited Hazim's mother to pay my respects, she seemed calm and at peace. She repeatedly said that her son was in heaven and that all would be well. I started to wonder how she could be at peace with this and how she could be so calm when strangers like me were shaken and devastated. Is it possible to find peace amid all this conflict, pain, and death?

As a teenager, I honestly didn't understand what peace felt like, because I had never been in a place of peace. I lived in a country torn by injustices and conflict. Peace was something hypothetical and out of reach—or so I thought.

For Palestinians, hearing gunshots was normal. Passing through multiple checkpoints and being searched as we went back and forth to school or work were all too familiar parts of our lives. Having soldiers surround our houses in the middle of the night in search of a family member or having relatives arrested and tortured in prison was common. The conflict and war was right at our doorstep, and everyone seemed affected by it. Through all this, I wondered, *What is peace? And where does someone find it?*

I grew up right next to the birthplace of the Savior. I often saw the places where He was raised, where He suffered, and where He died. I could not understand why the Savior chose my country to be born in. He is the Creator of the world and could have chosen any city and any country to be born in. Why did He choose my country? Palestine seemed to be a place of conflict all the time. It had one invasion after another and definitely seemed to lack earthly peace. When Isaiah prophesied about the Savior, he called Him the Prince of Peace: "For unto us a child is born, unto us a son is given: and the government shall be upon his shoulder: and his name shall be called Wonderful, Counsellor, The mighty God, The everlasting Father, The Prince of Peace" (Isaiah 9:6). So why would someone referred to as the Prince of Peace choose to be born in Palestine, a place of constant conflict and war?

I was raised in a town where, two thousand years ago, angels appeared to shepherds to inform them that their Savior had been born in Bethlehem. An angel proclaimed to the shepherds: "Fear not: for, behold, I bring you good tidings of great joy, which shall be to all people. For unto you is born this day in the city of David a Saviour, which is Christ the Lord. And this shall be a sign unto you; Ye shall find the babe wrapped in swaddling clothes, lying in a manger" (Luke 2:10–12).

That initial message from the angel to the shepherds was followed by a multitude of heavenly hosts praising God: "Glory to God in the highest, and on earth *peace,* good will toward men" (Luke 2:14; emphasis added). Peace on earth? But peace surely did not seem to exist in my country. So what is this peace the angels were referring to?

I discovered the answer to this question when I began investigating the Church. After I repented of my sins and started obeying the commandments, I started experiencing peace. This was a strange feeling to me, something I had never before experienced. It was a simple feeling that developed within me as I changed my heart, repented of my sins, and followed Jesus Christ. It was a warm feeling that engulfed my heart and soul, comforted me, and brought deep joy. It was a feeling that brought nourishment to a soul that had been hungry for years. Peace came into my life the minute I decided to walk in the footsteps of the Prince of Peace. Right after I joined the Church, I wrote in my journal: "My country has never experienced peace, but now I feel my heart has enough peace to cover the entire country of Palestine and to cover all the pain and suffering of my people."

Sometimes when I look back on my life, I can't help but think of a roller coaster. I love riding roller coasters. One of my favorite roller coasters at an amusement park in Utah drops 90 degrees from the top. The rush and thrill of going to the top and then dropping down is amazing. The worst part of a roller coaster ride is moving slowly upward, not knowing when the drop will happen. You fear that drop, but you look forward to it at the same time.

In a way, my life has been one big roller coaster. I have had major trials and sometimes a rough, shaky ride. But, as I look back at my life, I know I have enjoyed every minute, even the big scary drops. If I were to do it all over, I would not change a thing.

We each waited a long time to come to earth. We shouted for joy when the plan of salvation was presented and probably looked forward to the ride of mortality. Just like people who hold on with both hands in a roller coaster, screaming all the way, there are some who pass through this journey of mortality complaining and not enjoying the many blessings that are available all around them.

I testify that we have a Savior who gave His life for us so that we could make it safely through this earthly life. He suffered so we would not have to. He calls us all to come unto Him, and He shares our burdens and lifts us. The Savior repeatedly tells us, "How often would I have gathered thy children together, even as a hen gathereth her chickens under her wings, and ye would not!" (Matthew 23:37). He wants to save us, He wants to succor us, and He wants to lift us and give us strength.

In my darkest hours, His light has helped me see. During the times when my feeble feet could not move any further, He carried me. As I went through rocky paths and thorny ways, the Lord knew the journey was necessary so He encircled me with His love and His Spirit warmed my heart.

I am grateful for every event in my life—good or bad. I have learned so much from what I have been through. Most of all, my life has taught me to appreciate what a big difference Christ can make in a person's life. He has surely made a difference in mine. I changed from being a depressed and hopeless individual into someone who is grateful to be alive. I have found the peace that my county has been striving for since 1948, and that peace comes from inside my heart. This peace comes through the Savior, who said, "In the world ye shall have tribulation: but be of good cheer; I have overcome the world" (John 16:33). This kind of peace will never be found at a negotiation table!

For more than sixty years, everyone in my country—and I, as well—had been looking for peace in the wrong place. We were trying to accomplish peace by gaining freedom and escaping the war all around us. However, I have come to realize that peace will not come from signing a treaty, nor through a demonstration, nor by breaking chains and achieving victory. There is one source for peace, and that is He who said, "Peace I leave with you, my peace I give unto you: not as the world giveth, give I unto you. Let not your heart be troubled, neither let it be afraid" (John 14:27). Jesus Christ clearly tells us that His peace is different; His peace is not the common peace everyone thinks of.

The peace our Savior offers is a special kind of peace. The words of the angels were, "And on earth peace, good will toward men." In the Arabic Bible, the last part of that sentence, "good will toward men," says, "*wa fi ennas al masarra*," which literally means "joy be in the people." I think

One of the houses affected by the bombing in Beit Sahour.

this clarifies that the peace and joy offered by the Savior are internal, not external. It is an emotional rather than a physical peace that He offers—a spiritual, internal peace.

I have come to realize that one of the reasons Christ was born in a place of conflict and constant war is to show us that real peace can come only through Him. The peace He offers is a kind of peace that is not dependent on the situation around us. It is not "as the world" would offer. The Prince of Peace has the power to stop wars and conflicts and to bring physical peace, but sometimes what is even more amazing is that He can and does provide internal peace to people living in difficult situations.

I remember one day when an Israeli helicopter was bombing some areas in my town of Beit Sahour. It was in response to gunshots fired at the Israeli army camp east of my town. The missiles fired by the helicopter must have hit a power cord, because the electricity went out in the entire town and the phones stopped working. We were worried because we did not know which houses were being targeted and if our relatives and friends in Beit Sahour were safe. My parents and I went up to the roof so we could see which areas in my town were affected. In the pitch-black darkness, all we could see was the glow of the missiles as they exploded in the far distance. My whole countenance shook as I heard the sound of each explosion.

I left my parents on the roof and took a flashlight down the dark stairway and into my room. After turning off the flashlight, I knelt down in the darkness and pled with Heavenly Father for comfort. I was concerned about my relatives and about others in my town whose homes were being attacked. As I began to pray, I felt an amazing peace come over me. There in the darkness of my room, with the sounds of gunshots and bombs around me, I was able to find peace. Heavenly Father comforted me and reassured me that my relatives and others in my town were going to be protected.

I testify that peace is possible. Internal peace is not dependent on the circumstances around us. This is the peace the Master offers. He gives this peace freely to anyone who is willing to come unto Him and follow Him. His peace cannot be taken away from us except by our own disobedience. I was able to have personal peace even while living in a place of constant turmoil and conflict. I believe that the only way to have peace in any country is through forgiveness, love, and respect for others.

When we choose to follow the Savior and obey His commandments, we can find peace and happiness. We may still live in a place with barriers, checkpoints, and restrictions, but we can feel liberated by His Atonement. He is the only one who can free us, both literally and spiritually. He has the power to remove all the barriers between us and Heavenly Father. He removes the chains of sin that bind us down, and He sets us free.

Happiness depends on who you are and who you are striving to become. It has nothing to do with what you have or where you live. We are told that "wickedness never was happiness" (Alma 41:10). This tells us that the way to happiness is righteousness. When we are at peace with ourselves, with God, and with others, we can feel happy. When we are striving to become the person that Heavenly Father wants us to become and are walking on the right path, we can be happy. When Lehi partook of the fruit of the tree of life, his soul was filled "with exceedingly great joy" (1 Nephi 8:12). That tree is not found only at the end of our path when we finally reach heaven. It is found at the start of our path when we get baptized and promise to follow the Savior. We can partake of this fruit and bring joy to our lives every step of the way as we repent and become more obedient. Every righteous choice we make, every act of service we do, every step we take along the straight and narrow path can bring joy to our souls. Happiness is not a destination; it is a way of life.

I testify that the Savior is the Prince of Peace. He is the only source of true peace and light in this dark world. If we come unto Him, we will find a joy and peace that we have never before experienced. If we turn our lives to Him and allow Him to be in charge of our lives, He will walk with us and often carry us back to His mansions above. I testify that the more obedient I have been, the happier I have felt. The blessings I have received through my obedience were feelings of comfort, peace, and joy. Although oftentimes our obedience will not bring us relief from trials, it does bring blessings and internal peace. Of this I bear witness.

I testify that Heavenly Father lives and that we are all His beloved sons and daughters. The Savior walked out of the tomb in Jerusalem on the third day and conquered death. He conquered misery, hopelessness, despair, sin, and all the chains that bind us. He lives! And because of Him, we can live again. Because of Him, we can find joy and peace and happiness in this life.

This book is far from being finished. One day I will seal it and return it to my Savior when I see Him again. For this book belongs to Him, just as my life belongs to him. I testify that our Savior does live and that He stands outside your door, waiting for you to open it. I am so grateful that I had the privilege of walking where He walked and living where He lived every day of my life. However, you don't need to live in Palestine to have Christ's light and peace inside your heart. All you need to do is follow Him. When you do, you will find a kind of happiness and joy unlike any you have ever experienced.

A BRIEF HISTORY OF PALESTINE FROM THE TIME OF CHRIST

1150 BC Palestine referred to in hieroglyphics of the 20th Dynasty in Egypt as being a part of the land of Canaan.

1000 BC–63 BC Palestine came under the rule of various Canaanitic kingdoms for short periods of time. Hebrews, Nebateans, Jebusites, Arameans, Philistines, and others created small kingdoms that were often at conflict with each other and occasionally conquered by or pledged allegiance to Egyptians or Persian empires.

63 BC–AD 330 The Romans ruled over Palestine. As a result of the Jewish Revolt (AD 66–70), the Romans besieged Jerusalem and destroyed the temple. In AD 135, the Roman emperor Hadrian made Jerusalem a Roman colony called Aelia Capitolina and established a pagan temple to Jupiter on the temple mount. The land was still called Palestine.

330–634 Palestine became part of the Roman Byzantine Empire in 330. With the capital in Byzantium, renamed Constantinople after the emperor Constantine (today's Istanbul in western Turkey), the empire's official religion became Christianity.

634–1096 Palestine became part of the Arab-Muslim Empire in 634, alternately ruled by the Seljuk Turks, the Umayyads from Damascus, and the Abbasids from Baghdad. Native inhabitants of Palestine were free to convert to Islam or remain Christians or Jews. Near the end of the seventh century, the Umayyad caliph constructed the Dome of the Rock and Al Aqsa mosque. For more than 1,400 years, therefore, the temple mount has been known by its Arab name, *Haram al-Sharif,* or "Noble Sanctuary."

1096–1517 Jerusalem was conquered by the Crusaders, Christian soldiers from Western Europe, who massacred all the Jews and Muslims in the city when they entered. In 1187, Saladin's army overthrew the Crusaders in Jerusalem, leading to a more than 300-year rule by Mamluk dynasties (slave-soldiers of primarily Turkish descent).

1517–1917 Ottoman Turks conquered Palestine from the Mamluks. The first official wave of Jewish immigration from Europe began in 1881, nearly doubling the Jewish population there to about 60,000 by the end of World War I (about 9 percent of the total population of Palestine at the time).

1917–1947 By the end of World War I, British, French, and Arab troops overthrew Turkish and German troops to free Palestine from Ottoman control. Britain was assigned responsibility over Palestine, and France took responsibility over Syria. The British Balfour Declaration of 1917 mandated Palestine as an official homeland for the Jewish people and pledged Britain's support for Zionist aspirations.

In part, the British Mandate read: "His Majesty's government view with favor the establishment in Palestine of a national home for the Jewish people, and will use their best endeavors to facilitate the achievement of this object, it being clearly understood that nothing shall be done which may prejudice the civil and religious rights of existing non-Jewish communities in Palestine or the rights and political status enjoyed by Jews in any other country."

Subsequently, British government talks considered the creation of two official states in the land: one for the Jews and the other for the Arabs. These talks included setting limits on Jewish immigration to mitigate the social conflict without negating the intent of the Balfour Declaration.

1947–1949 To replace the Balfour Declaration, a United Nations commission outlined recommendations to partition the land of Palestine into two separate states. The United Nations general assembly recommended partition with the boundaries for a Jewish state consisting of 55 percent of the land for the Jews and 45 percent of the land for the Arabs. At the time, Jews (mostly new immigrants) comprised less than a third of the population and owned less than 7 percent of the land. Jerusalem and its environs were to be an "international zone" and, therefore, were not assigned to either the Jewish or Arab state. Ultimately, the Jews in Palestine embraced the plan that allotted them nearly ten times the land they had previously owned while the Palestinian Arabs rejected it.

14 May 1948 The British Mandate ended, and an official State of Israel was proclaimed. Civil war resulted, with multiple attacks and counterattacks, including the massacre of Deir Yassin, an entire Palestinian village of men, women, and children. In retaliation, a convoy of Jewish medical personnel was destroyed. The next seven months witnessed the concerted efforts of armies from Jordan, Syria, Egypt, Lebanon, and Iraq attacking Israel in an attempt to destroy it before it could take root. In a few places, like Jerusalem and Nazareth, Arab residents were allowed to stay in their homes and thus became residents of Israel. However, amid the conflict, tens of thousands were designated as refugees and housed in camps in their own country and surrounding countries. At the time of the January 1949 cease-fire, Israel had expanded its territory from 55 percent of the land to 77 percent. The last remaining Arab territory, the West Bank, was thereafter annexed to Jordan.

June 1967 *The Six-Day War.* Continual clashes between Israel and the surrounding Arab nations escalated when President Gamal Abdel Nasser of Egypt closed the Gulf of Aqaba to shipping, which Israel interpreted as a declaration of war. Israel struck an Egyptian airbase while their planes were still grounded and within a week occupied the Gaza Strip and Sinai (territories ruled by Egypt), Syria's Golan Heights, and the West Bank and the Old City of Jerusalem. In November of that year, the Security Council Resolution #242 was issued, which called for Israel to withdraw from all the Palestinian territories of the recent conflict and for the Arab nations to recognize Israel's right to exist as an official and independent state. The resolution has largely been ignored as successive Israeli governments have persisted in building Israeli settlements throughout the West Bank to disconnect Palestinian communities and establish a permanent Jewish presence there.

April 1971 Sahar was born.

1987–1993 *The First Intifada ("Uprising").* After twenty years of Israeli occupation, a spontaneous protest among Palestinians in the West Bank and the Gaza Strip erupted. Sparked by news of a line of Palestinian workers who were killed when a truck driven by an Israeli purposely rammed into them, Palestinian boys and young men took to the streets to demonstrate their frustration and anger. Some threw stones and petrol bombs at Israeli occupation soldiers, but most of the uprising participants used nonviolent strategies inspired by those practiced in other countries before. Israeli soldiers responded with violence and systematic torture of captive Palestinians. Some 1,100 Palestinians were killed by Israeli forces, and many more were killed by Israeli settlers living in the West Bank. Some 20,000 more were injured. This widespread outcry from young Palestinians was heard, resulting in the recognition of the State of Palestine by 55 countries.

1993 *The Oslo Peace Accord.* As a result of secret negotiations in Norway, Israeli Prime Minister Yitzhak Rabin and Palestinian leader Yasser Arafat signed an agreement to allow for an interim creation of a "Palestinian National Authority" in the West Bank and Gaza. The accord outlined gradual Israeli withdrawal and the hope was that the five-year accord would lead to a Palestinian state in those areas (22% of historic Palestine). But in practice, Palestinians had control over only a tiny part of the land, and Israel used this accord to build more settlements, so that between 1993 and 2000 the population of the Jewish settlers in the area that was to become a Palestinian state tripled.

2000–2004 *The Second Intifada.* On September 28, 2000, the soon-to-be Israeli Prime Minister Ariel Sharon visited a Muslim holy site, the *Haram al-Sharif.* A thousand Israeli security personnel accompanied him as he declared that Israel would never forfeit its claims to Jerusalem or the "Temple Mount." The Second Intifada erupted as Palestinians again took to the streets to protest. An estimated 3,000 Palestinians and 1,000 Israelis lost their lives. The second Palestinian uprising also led to more Israeli checkpoints and blockades on roads that connected Palestinian villages and cities and to prolonged curfews and closed schools.

2002–present *The Building of the Separation Wall.* In 2002, Israel started constructing the separation wall that surrounds the West Bank and encircles some Palestinian cities. Over 1.5 million fruiting trees were uprooted in order to build the wall. These were trees that had sustained Palestinian families for generations.

Sources

Colin Chapman, *Whose Promised Land? The Continuing Crisis over Israel and Palestine* (Baker Books: Grand Rapids, Mich., 2002).

Mazin B. Qumsiyeh, *Sharing the Land of Canaan: Human Rights and the Israeli-Palestine Struggle* (Pluto Press: London, 2004).